The Utah Batteries
During the Spanish-American War

The Utah Batteries
During the Spanish-American War

Charles R. Mabey

LEONAUR

The Utah Batteries During the Spanish-American War
by Charles R. Mabey

Originally published in 1900 under the title:
The Utah Batteries: a History
A Complete Account of the Muster-In, Sea Voyage, Battles, Skirmishes and
Barrack Life of the Utah Batteries, Together With Biographies of Officers
and Muster-Out Rolls.

Leonaur is an imprint of Oakpast Ltd

Material original to this edition and presentation of the
text in this form copyright © 2011 Oakpast Ltd

ISBN: 978-0-85706-629-9 (hardcover)
ISBN: 978-0-85706-630-5 (softcover)

http://www.leonaur.com

Publisher's Notes

Contents

To the Utah Batterymen

who bravely fought for their country's flag on
a foreign soil, this book is respectfully
dedicated by the author

Preface

Sometime after the Utah Battalion left San Francisco for the Philippines the author conceived the idea of writing a history of that organization after its return from the war. With this purpose in view he kept a diary during the entire campaign and also collected what other material that could be utilized for such a work. Immediately upon the arrival in Salt Lake City of the discharged volunteers he, with others, set to work to bring about a completion of this plan. This little volume represents the result of the labour expended at intervals between that date and the present time. The author claims no more for it than its title assumes—a brief history of the Utah batteries. It is no more. There may be some works in the future which will command, to a greater extent, the attention of the reading public. This is not written with the idea that it will become a standard work, but that while those events which happened are yet green in the memories of the Utah artillerymen, they may be recorded and not be consigned to oblivion. The author trusts he may not be asserting too much when he affirms that the book is written with a strict adherence to facts, as he has had access both to public and private data in the compiling of the work, and he has been scrupulously careful in guarding against errors of every description. At this opportunity he takes pleasure in thanking those officers and men who have helped him in bringing about an accomplishment of his plans, and furthermore, he wishes to extend his thanks to Angus K. Nicholson for his contributions and a like communication to those friends who have given him timely advice and aid in disposing of difficulties which have arisen from time to time.

Introduction

The history of the Utah Batteries should be a plain tale, for deeds of valour cannot be garnished by the flower of rhetoric or the pomp of oratory. This is a simple story of brave deeds. The stern browed Heracles standing unarmed in the midst of his countrymen was a frank, common figure, but when he dashed like Ares upon the Lerneaen hydra he became majestic, and no mere pen picture could augment his greatness. So we shall paint a picture of the achievements of the cannoneers and gunners of Utah while withstanding the onslaughts of the dusky warriors of Aguinaldo, and no greater compliment can be paid them than a clear true narrative of their exploits.

Utah was early distinguished in the furious fights of Luzon. Even before the soldiers of "Uncle Sam" had felt their way into the defences of Manila, her guns had awaked the long-sleeping sentries of the Dons and torn holes into the bulwarks of Spanish oppression and tyranny. Her later accomplishments against the fierce Tagalan braves have only served to increase the homage and admiration of the world, yet, in the dark days of the conflict, as veterans know, are performed many daring acts and feats of human strength, which are never recorded in the chronicles of fame, or proclaimed by the bugle's blare. There were those who knew what it was to feel the pangs of hunger and the ravages of disease, those who experienced the racking pains occasioned by fatiguing marches, and long, weary tramps through the unbroken wilderness of the tropics; and there were belated ones who hid in the swamps anxiously watching for the first beams of dawn to reveal the lurking foe.

An account of the actions of the men of Utah is not a recital of the performances of one man; neither is it a description of the doings of a particular section of men. It is the story of brave men fighting under competent chiefs. Their history is exceptional. In every engagement against the insurrectionists, on land and river, the unceasing fire of the guns of Utah was heard. While Major Young, Major Grant, Captain Critchlow and Lieutenant Seaman battered down the enemy's breastworks at Caloocan and San Lazerus cemetery, the cannon under Captain Wedgewood hurled fiery wrath into the terrified foe at Sampaloe, and Lieutenant Webb's death-dealing monsters flung destruction into the ranks of the Filipino hordes at Santa Mesa. While the land batteries, with the infantry, worked their way through the tropical forests in that campaign which drove the natives out of Calumpit and San Fernando and sent Aguinaldo flying into the mountains beyond, Major Grant, Lieutenant Naylor and Lieutenant Webb, with their fire-spitting dragons, the river gunboats, bore down upon the insurgents at Morong and Santa Cruz and disturbed the silence of the primitive woods at San Luiz and Candaba.

The country was not slow in recognizing Utah. Almost as soon as hostilities commenced Major Young was elevated to a position on General MacArthur's staff, and when the river gunboats were put into commission in anticipation of a Tagalan outbreak Lieutenant R. C. Naylor was placed second in command. Later when the river fleet was enlarged Major Grant took command and Lieutenant William C. Webb assumed control of the *Covadonga*, positions which both held till Utah's fighting days were over.

The Utah cannoneers were not only exceptional as fighters, but they did things before unheard of in artillery annals. They pushed along in line with the infantry in many a hard-fought encounter in the vanguard; during the early days of the conflict, when the rival force first turned its weapons upon the walls of Manila, they hauled their pieces after them in grim pursuit of the fleeing foe. They stood comparison with the well-drilled regulars, and in many instances surpassed them; the bark of their iron-tongued guns never failed to strike terror into the hearts of the dusky braves of Luzon, while it ever sounded as a note of cheer to the infantrymen on the straggling skirmish line.

There is Santa Mesa, Malabon, Quingua, Bag Bag, San Fernando—words hollow sounding to the ordinary ear; but when named to the stalwart veteran they touch a chord which quickens the pulse and sets every nerve fibre vibrating with emotion. To him each tells a tale of noble achievements wrought beneath the broiling sun of the tropics; to him each whispers an assurance that his duty was bravely done in the blasting fires of the East.

The warriors of Utah have listened to their last reveille and their last retreat. When they withdrew from the Orient they left the scenes of carnage behind and returned to loved ones and to peace. May that peace be lasting and happy.

CHAPTER 1

The Mustering

When the war trumpet's shrill notes disturbed the serenity of
this tranquil land early in '98 their echoes were not lost on the hills
of Utah, but reverberating from cliff to cliff and peak to peak they
swelled into a martial hymn whose chorus was sung in every home
in the commonwealth. The dark stormy days preceding the declaration of war in April had aroused the dormant energies of men,
hitherto engaged in the peaceful pursuits of life, and filled them
with an eager desire to perform the more exciting duties of the
camp, so that when the call was issued by Governor Wells on April
25th a host of young men from every corner of the State applied
for enlistment in the volunteer army.

Out of the 500 men, Utah's original quota, 343 were designated for the Light Artillery service. There are reasons for this not
altogether understood by those outside military circles. At the
breaking out of hostilities with Spain the National Guard of the
various States were deficient in this branch of the service. The
guns consisted mostly of obsolete and useless muzzle-loading
cannon, divided among the States at the close of the Civil War.
Some were smooth bores, others rifled. There were Napoleons
and Parrots, brass cannon and twenty-four pounders. Very few of
the States had modern guns, but Utah was especially favoured in
this line. During the early organization of the guard she had been
provided with eight 3.2-inch B. & L. rifles, together with limbers,
caisson, harnesses, etc. Thus it was apparent to all who knew anything of the manner of procedure that the youngest State in the
Union would be called upon to furnish artillery, and so it proved,
for, after having been informed by Senator Frank J. Cannon that

this State could man the guns, the War Department made arrangements for Utah to put two batteries in the field.

The day following the governor's call recruiting officers were appointed to enlist men for the service, the names of those designated to enrol batterymen being Richard W. Young, Frank A. Grant, George W. Gibbs, Ray C. Naylor and Orrin R. Grow. These were assigned to different portions of the State and the work began on the day following. Ethan Allen, afterwards first sergeant of Battery A, was the first man to enrol. Orders were received from Washington naming Fort Douglas as the rendezvous for the recruits, the message reaching here the day enlistment began. Briant H. Wells, a lieutenant in the Second United States Infantry, who had been stationed here on duty with the National Guard, was assigned as mustering officer. The recruiting continued with varied success until May 1st, when the quota was filled. Applications for enrolment were so plentiful after the news of the call became generally known that recruiting officers were frequently compelled to have the men draw lots in order to determine the lucky ones, for that is the term then used.

May 3rd, camps were pitched on the lower parade ground at Fort Douglas. It was named Camp Kent in honour of Colonel (now major-general, retired) J. Ford Kent, who had commanded the Twenty-fourth United States Infantry stationed at the fort when hostilities were declared, and which had marched away but a short time before. As soon as the camp was established the men began coming in. It was a strange gathering of men which appeared at the surgeon's door for examination the following morning. Farmers fresh from the plough, cowboys from the plain, miners from the mountains, blacksmiths from the forge, students, teachers, doctors, bookkeepers had assembled to be defenders in common of the Nation's honour.

On May 4th the officers were selected. The appointments of the governor were as follows: *Battery A*—captain, R. W. Young; first lieutenant, George W. Gibbs; second lieutenants, Ray C. Naylor and Thomas B. Braby. Lieutenant Braby declined the honour and William C. Webb was selected in his stead. *Battery B*—captain, Frank A. Grant; first lieutenant, Edgar A. Wedgewood; second lieutenants, John F. Critchlow and Orrin R. Grow.

These selections were regarded as very happy ones. Captain Young is a graduate of West Point and was at one time a lieutenant in the Second United States Artillery; Lieutenant Gibbs was the major commanding the battalion of light artillery in the National Guard of Utah; Lieutenant Naylor was one of the founders of the National Guard and had worked his way up to a lieutenant-colonelcy, while Lieutenant Webb had been for some time the captain of Company A, First Infantry N.G.U.

All the officers of Battery B had been identified with the National Guard. Captain Grant was colonel of the First Regiment; Lieutenant Wedgewood was formerly captain of a company stationed at Provo; Lieutenant Critchlow was a member of the medical staff, while Lieutenant Grow was major of the first battalion of the First Infantry.

No time was lost after the officers had been chosen, as the work of disciplining the raw force immediately began. Camp Kent was the scene of bustle and hurry. It was drill, drill, drill, from morning until night, and "Action Front," "Action Right," "Action Left," "Change Posts," "Section left front into line" kept the men moving from reveille until retreat. All seemed anxious to become proficient in the use of the guns, and even guard duty—that task ever despised by the soldier—was performed with a surprising willingness.

On May 9th Lieutenant Wells administered the oath which transformed the body of citizens into a battalion of soldiers. The work of preparing the roll was cheerfully done and was accelerated somewhat by the arrival of a message from the War Department announcing that the Utah Batteries would be sent to the Philippines. The declaration was received with satisfaction by some, but others were less enthusiastic as an opinion prevailed that there would be no fighting in the East, but that Cuba would furnish the battles of the war. Later developments proved this to be a mistake, for long after the Spanish had felt the force of American war machinery at San Juan and El Caney their lost subjects in the Antipodes were fleeing in terror before the mighty thunder of the Utah guns at Santa Mesa and Bag Bag.

The batteries left for San Francisco on May 20th. It was an imposing sight to see the newly recruited soldiers, commanded by Captain Young, as they marched down the streets to the depot followed by thousands of citizens who gathered to bid them farewell. Some partings between relations were exceedingly touching and sad. Perhaps mothers and sisters, fathers and brothers read in the dim misty vista of the future the fate to which some of the men were doomed in the furious skirmishes of Luzon. Cheer after cheer rang out as the train pulled away and the volunteers responded with vigour, although there were some whose voices sounded husky as the final greetings were given.

On their arrival at San Francisco the batteries received a royal welcome, the Red Cross society taking especial pains to make their visit a pleasant one. Several weeks were consumed in perfecting the organization and preparing it for foreign service. Lieutenant Wedgewood and Sergeants Brown and Fehr returned to Utah and recruited 104 men to complete the organizations to their full strength, leaving Salt Lake City with them on June 29th. On June 15th the batteries sailed away to the land across the seas where work of a far more serious nature awaited them.

The voyage across was not altogether unlike a voyage on any ordinary vessel, save for the fact that the men were crowded a little closer than on a first-class passenger boat, and the food was not so elaborate in character as one would expect to find in a first grade hotel or a railway dining car. The men kicked in the good natured American way and continued to eat what was given them and slept as best they could.

A stop was made at Honolulu, where occurred a reception to the Utah men which marked a bright day in the life of the soldier. The transports arrived on the night of the 23rd, and at 11 o'clock. The next morning they went ashore amid the cheers of the Hawaiians, who gave them a greeting hearty and cordial. Flowers were in profusion and pretty girls threw bouquets at the tired pilgrims until they felt that they had indeed found the "Paradise of the Pacific." Judge Kinney, a former resident of Salt Lake City, headed the reception committee, and there were elaborate preparations to make the stay one of gladness. The great sugar works and plantations at Oahu were visited and the points of interest carefully shown. Then under the shading palms, amid the fragrance of flowers, with hundreds of pretty girls to wait on them the men sat down to the banquet. In an atmosphere which breathes poetry and pleasure; where the soft tropical zephyr kisses the cheek as a mother does a sleeping infant the choicest fruits were served and substantial edibles tempted the appetite. Soldiers made love to maidens with dusky cheeks; American blue eyes told short stories of love to Kanaka brown, and the Caucasian ladies were not forgotten, for it was a feast of love. Everywhere was *"Aloha, Aloha."*

But all things end. The next day saw the ships sail away. With the sweet fragrance of blossoms still lingering in their nostrils and the long-to-be-remembered clasp of friendship yet plainly felt they passed away from the dreamy isle into the oblivion of the Pacific to resume the diet of beef *a la* can and coal *a la* "Colon." Once more was ship soup staple and tropical sea monotony plentiful.

A few days later the fleet arrived at Wake Island, which General Greene took possession of in the name of the United States. Five days after this the Ladrone Islands were sighted and passed.

About the middle of the month the Philippines were sighted and on the 17th the fleet of transports entered the harbour of Manila escorted by the cruiser *Boston*.

The landing was an exceedingly difficult undertaking. The facilities for taking the guns from the transports were not perfect. The guns were put ashore in about five feet of water and had to be hauled out by hand, but the work was accomplished in the usual good natured American fashion, and when this task was finished men dried their clothes as though nothing had happened. In landing several amusing incidents occurred. Many Filipinos, anxious to earn a few *centavos*, flocked around the ships, and not a few of the men hired a native as a sort of a pack horse to carry them ashore. One two-hundred-pound soldier was unfortunate in the selection of his human pack horse, for he sat astride the shoulders of a ninety-pound native until the little fellow broke down and buried himself and rider in the sad sobbing sea waves to the great amusement of his comrades and his own disgust. Other occurrences were equally as ludicrous.

The several days following the landing of the batteries were spent in giving the men the rest they had earned and needed. No work worthy of mention was done until the morning of the 29th, when came the first scent of trouble—of war. From the actions of the officers at early morning it was plain to be seen that something was going to happen. Two guns of Battery A were taken over to the trenches which had been built by the insurgents near the Capuchin Monastery. During the day the sharpshooters of the Twenty-third United States Infantry and the Spanish had been doing some desultory firing with little result on either side, save that the men kept their heads closer to the breastworks, while a battalion of the Colorado Infantry, under Colonel Mc-Coy, advanced beyond the old trenches to a point near the monastery, where they threw up a new line of earthworks. The two guns of Battery A moved to this point the following morning and took possession of the emplacements already constructed. On the following morning two guns under Lieutenant Grow of Battery B were brought over from Camp Dewey and placed in position on the left. Men from both lines were engaged in erecting gun pits all along the front. The guns were located about 1000 yards from Fort San Antonio de Abad, which formed the extreme right of the Spanish line. The enemy's left and centre was protected by a line of entrenchments. Outpost duty was being performed by a company of the Eighteenth United States Infantry. The firing, which had been kept up with more or less vigour, came from the right of the Utah position, which was entirely unprotected owing to a failure on the part of the insurgents to maintain their lines between Calle Real and the Pasig road.

During the night of July 30th-31st the excitement began. Heavy small arm firing was indulged in by the enemy and from his lines came shells at irregular intervals, none of which did any damage. At this time Lieutenant Naylor was in the trenches with the two guns of Battery A. At 8 o'clock next morning Lieutenant Gibbs relieved him of the command with two-gun detachments of fresh men. All day everything was quiet. The enemy was planning a night attack, as he had no desire to mix with the American forces in a fair open fight in the broad light of day, but rather trusted to darkness to accomplish his designs. Everything was quiet until 11:30 that evening, when the Mausers began singing venomously from the Spanish lines. Then came the boom of his artillery and the men in the trenches knew that the time for action had come. The Tenth Pennsylvania troops replied with their Springfields and the whiz of the 45s mingled with the keen "twang" of the Mausers, while the Third Artillerymen, equipped as regular infantry, took a part in the altercation. The instructions of the Utah men were not to fire until it was evident the enemy was making an advance. The cannoneers stood by their guns awaiting the orders which should make them a part of the fight. Finally it came. Major Cuthberton of the First California, the senior officer present, gave the word and then Utah's voice was heard for the first time during the war. The gunners worked like Trojans and with shrapnel punched at zero they sent shell after shell into the Castilian lines. Corporal Charles Varian, with no clothing on save a pair of trousers, sweating like a man who was working for his life, yet cool withal, managed his piece like a veteran. Sergeant J. O. Nystrom gave orders in a collected way that instilled fresh courage into the hearts of his men. W. W. Riter wore a seraphic smile as he sighted his gun at the spits of flame on the other side, while Billy Kneass worked his cannon with the *sang froid* of a man in a blind waiting for ducks. It was a warm time and when morning dawned it was ascertained that several Castilian voices had been added to Choral Society in that land beyond the river. Utah's men were standing their baptism of fire and proved themselves soldiers. All the terrible passion of war had supplanted the first feelings of timidity, and they manipulated their guns with as much composure as they would have handled the pigskins on the gridiron. But the ammunition was running short. Fifty-seven shrapnel had been discharged and the battle was still on. The Pennsylvania men had fired away nearly all their ammunition, and affairs began to look serious, when a body of men from Camp Dewey hauling a limber chest after them dashed from out the gloom. Once more across the intervening space the shells shrieked and broke the Spanish lines, causing havoc and terror. The attempt of the "Dons" had proved futile, and after having fought for two and a half hours they withdrew.

Although other commands had lost men the Utah boys were fortunate in this that not one of their number was killed and only one slightly wounded in this engagement.

For several days but little was done by the Utah troops. The men constructed emplacements for the guns, cut down timber which might have interfered with good work and awaited orders.

In the meantime the lieutenants of the batteries were relieving each other from day to day. The fire from the Spanish lines was kept up in a desultory manner and was replied to by the infantry in the American lines.

The final engagement on the 13th was short, but the guns of the Utah men did wonderful execution. In conjunction with Dewey's fleet they tore holes in the Spanish fort at Malate and helped in forcing the enemy out of his position on the extreme left.

CHAPTER 2

Barrack Life

Like all the other organizations which had taken part in the capturing of Manila, the Utah batteries were without a home when they first entered the city. Battery A found temporary quarters in a spacious *nipa* hut in the Malate district, while Battery B went into barracks in the Odministracion de Hacienda. Several days later Major Young secured the Cuartel de Meisic, formerly occupied by a Spanish engineer regiment, and Battery A was stationed there August 18th. Some days following Battery B moved into the same building. The Third Artillery occupied the south half of the Cuartel, and the batteries were domiciled in the east and west wings of the north half. The Cuartel was a large and stalwart structure located in the most picturesque part of Manila. South of it lay the business portion of Manila, with its Escolta, its Plaza de Cervantes, and its Hotel de Oriente; to the west was the Marcadero teeming with rustic Filipino maids and redolent with its Oriental odours; stretching away to the north were the broad rice fields and forests of bamboo, with the mountains in the distance forming a background. It was a pleasant home and one which the men appreciated.

During the first few weeks of barrack life the men settled down serene in the thought that they would soon be speeding homeward. Their duty had been done and they felt that they were now entitled to the happier pleasures of Utah. But days passed, and were lengthened into weeks, weeks passed and were lengthened into months, and still they remained in the tropics with less hope of returning home than they had at first entertained. The novelty of their surroundings began to wear off and everything which the

Philippines could afford became decidedly commonplace. Unable, therefore, to find other entertainments when off duty, as a pastime the men exchanged reminiscent fairy tales about their late combat. Wearying of these occupations they often sauntered out of the Cuartel in bodies in quest of what little mirth they could get out of the passive and inexplicable natives.

Of course, there were drills and everybody liked them, as they produced such an excellent opportunity for one to give vent to his feelings after the drills were over with. Those were happy hours which the men spent in sweltering under the genial warmth of the southern sun, and learning with a bitter vengeance the tactics of "dismounted drill." And "double time," too, was always a pleasant innovation as it generated a bodily heat to correspond with mental feelings and external influences. Then there was always an appreciative audience of gaping nut-brown maids and matrons who took delight in watching the *soldado* go through his ever-changing evolutions. Yes, those were days which the veteran will always look back upon with rapture.

At first some trouble was occasioned over the inadequate food supply; but that difficulty was soon obliterated. The then acting commissary sergeant was removed and A. L. Williams, familiarly known among his admirers in the battalion by the euphonious prefixes of "Dad" and "Judge," was elevated to this position. Under the judicious management of the Judge a revolution was made in the department and the men waxed fat from the overflowing cornucopia of the commissary.

In those murky days of Manila were other things which served to offset the oppressive blazonry of the tropic sun. In order to make the attire of the soldiers harmonize as much as possible with the requirements of the climate, light shirts and trousers were provided by the quartermaster's department. Every week occurred a general inspection, to which the men were expected to appear housed in this startling white with polished shoes and flaming brass buckles. A very imposing appearance they made when lined up on these occasions.

The advent of the soldier vastly accelerated the trade of the native fruit vendors in the vicinity of the Cuartel, and as time wore on this peculiar product of the Orient increased his sales by the addition of the deadly *vino*, sometimes with rather disastrous results to the imbiber. That wondrous monument of human ingenuity commonly known as "army hardtack" formed the standard medium of exchange between the industrious fruit dealer and his overworked customer. The barred windows of the Cuartel became the market ground for all the products of Luzon, and through them many a luscious mango was exchanged for an adamantine biscuit upon which the soldier had vainly expended all his dental energy. The natives had full access to the barracks at this time, and the native washerwoman made the *blanco* trousers shine iridescently for inspection by beating them against the sunny side of a boulder and afterwards pressing them with a fearfully and wonderfully made flatiron.

Hard by the Cuartel were a number of *tiendas*, widely known among the soldiers as *vino* stands. The presiding spirit over one of these establishments was generally a pretty *mestiza*, who, in addition to her natural charms, was blessed with a high-sounding Castilian name. There were four shops run on the plan, which held pre-eminence both for the character of the *vin* which they supplied and the bewitching charms of their owners. The returned volunteer will remember with keen enjoyment Juanita, Juaquina, Victoriana and above all Isabella, the saintly and virtuous, who was equally as skilful in obtaining the nimble sixpence as in raising a brood of *mestiza* children. There was also "Madre," withered and antiquated, but a born dictator, and through her superior management she came to be known as the top-sergeant. Finally there was Ysabel, with a gentle smile upon her pleasant brunette face, and Estepania, brown-eyed and plump, most beautiful among all the *mestiza* belles. Isabella's casa was the place to which the eyes of the weary soldier turned after a long and fatiguing drill; afterwards it was the point to which his footsteps inevitably led when he was able to rush in for a few days from the firing line. The house was large and spacious, with polished ebony floors and wide windows through which the balmy zephyrs blew and kissed the heated brow of the tired fighter. Beautiful creepers twisted their way up the wall and stole in at the extensive balcony to catch a taste of the pleasures within; the broad-leafed banana palm surrounded the casa and broke the power of the blazing tropic sun. It was, indeed, the one spot in all the East which made the home-loving Utahns feel at home. When away all his secret longings were centred upon that place and its attractions, and his mouth yearned for a renewed acquaintance with the delicate omelettes fashioned by the dainty fingers of Pania and the crab brought from the bay by the ubiquitous Peek-a-boo. His mind reverted with gratitude to the anxious solicitations of "Madre" when she learned that he was suffering from a headache and he acutely remembered the healing balm which she applied to his fevered brow. He knew, too, that should he be struck down in death by the bullet of the enemy, what tears of sympathy would be shed at the news of his misfortune.

A FAMILIAR SCENE

The one source of worriment about the Isabella mansion was the fact that the thirsty soldiers were frequently given an over supply of the deadly *vino*. Such an occurrence was attended with dire results; but as the motherly "Madre" was blessed with an abundant store of remedies, under her care the victim was soon restored to his mental equilibrium. All soldiers seem gifted with special powers to spend money and as a consequence few of them could command the attention of a penny bootblack twenty-four hours after being paid, but this weakness had no weight with the kindly old dame who carried a large credit roll and could refuse nothing to a Utah soldado. So Isabella's mansion forms a part of the war history of the Utah batteries; and it must be remembered with other and more stirring scenes; for when the thoughts of the Utah soldier stray to the domicile of the Isabella family they are mingled with happy reminiscences and strange memories and tragic sights.

*   *   *   *   *

One hundred and four weary and footsore recruits arrived in the Cuartel on the 28th of August and deposited their blankets and all other portable property on the greensward. They had been waiting out in the bay four days and had finally reached the Cuartel after having made a complete circuit of the city. Sergeant Arthur W. Brown piloted the new batch of volunteers to their home, and ever since the redoubtable sergeant has borne a reputation, as a file leader, which would make a Mexican burro grow green-eyed with envy.

Here it might be stated that after watching the fleet of transports, which conveyed the Utah batteries, sail out of the rugged Golden Gate into the broad Pacific, Lieutenant E. A. Wedgewood and Sergeants Arthur W. Brown and L. N. Fehr turned toward Utah bent on the mission of securing 104 recruits, which would give each battery its full quota of 173. Volunteers were numerous but the work of enlisting covered a period of nine days. Recruits were obtained from all points in the State but the majority came from Salt Lake City. On the 28th of June the full number had been enrolled and the following day the small body of men left for San Francisco, after being accorded a warm demonstration at the depot. At Oakland they remained all night of the 30th and the following morning they marched to Camp Merritt, from which place they were removed to the Presidio two days later.

Late in June Lieutenant Wedgewood was taken ill with typhoid fever but remained with the men until July 6th, when he was taken to the Lane hospital and Lieutenant Diss of the California Heavy Artillery was placed temporarily in charge of the recruits. Orders were for the Utah contingent to sail on the transport *Rio de Janeiro*, and as the South Dakota Infantry was the only organization on the vessel Lieutenant Foster of that regiment was given command of the men.

The voyage was uneventful save that the soldiers were ill-treated by Lieutenant Foster, who succeeded in gaining for himself the eternal hatred of the men under his charge. As the recruits were then unacquainted with military practices, many expressions of disgust being made in an unguarded way, reached the ears of the worthy lieutenant, who heaped still greater indignities upon the men by way of retaliation.

At Honolulu W. A. Kinney, the large plantation owner, entertained the Utahns during their brief stay in that city.

The *Rio de Janeiro* arrived in Manila Bay on the 24th of August, but it was four days later before the recruits set foot on the soil of Luzon and made their phenomenal march up the streets of Manila to Plaza de Felipe II, where they greeted their comrades.

Lieutenant Wedgewood, having recovered from his fever, arrived October 4th on the *Scandia*, which left San Francisco on August 27th.

During the long dreary days following the arrival of the recruits their life was not entirely joyous. From sunrise to sunset they were forced to listen to the blood-curdling tales which their companions told of the late conflict with the "Dons." At first they hearkened to them with respectful attention. They never doubted the truth of these glowing fairy stories. They revered these self-lauding heroes as a species of immortal beings. In return for this tributary deference they were treated with contempt. The veteran called them "rookies," and whenever one of them attempted to soar he was promptly and sternly reminded of his inferiority and kindly invited to get off the pedestal upon which he had so unwittingly placed himself while one of his superiors proceeded to relate a harrowing tale of blood and thunder and rain down in the trenches. Every bit of rainy weather or glorious sunset reminded the Malate hero of something he had seen in the trenches and at once he began to dilate upon it with great attention to details and a lofty air of his own importance.

So it went on. The recruits vainly sought for relief. He tried to stem the tide of persecution by relating stories of his own. But as soon as he made such an attempt he was immediately "bawled out" and his tormentors proceeded with a fresh tirade. Finally one of the groaning victims hit upon a happy plan, and after it was carried out it effectually stopped the torture. When in the future the mendacious veteran essayed to array himself in a cloud of glory by narrating legends of personal prowess, he was unceremoniously suppressed by the rookies, who sang:

It may be so; I do not know,
But it sounds to me like a lie.

Instantly upon the starting of this little hymn it was taken up by every soldier in the barracks and the unlucky veteran, crestfallen and beaten, was only too glad to retire into seclusion.

*   *   *   *   *

During those five months in which the soldier was learning the peculiarities of Oriental life and sweltering under the rays of the Southern sun, he adopted any means of causing the speedy destruction of time. After the singularities of his new surroundings had ceased to be uncommon he began to look about himself in search of other amusement. Naturally a person who adapts himself easily to his environments, he took up with the games of the Filipinos, and, as a consequence, soon after the appearance of the American as a prominent figure on the streets of Manila, it was no unusual occurrence to behold the huge, good-natured Yankee engaged in friendly sport with the diminutive and fiery Tagalan.

As cock-fighting is the national game of the native the soldier seized upon this diversion with an enthusiasm that was truly remarkable. The slender and wiry game cock was in great demand. The feathered pugilist became the hero of the hour. The price of *pollos* jumped above par two or three times over. On the shady side of every street could be seen little knots of men eagerly awaiting the outcome of a battle in which these kings among all the fowl tribe were engaged. And the victory was not decided without great loss, for frequently the champion proclaimed himself conqueror by mounting the gory body of his late enemy and crowing with great vigour. Men bet on their favourites with as much fervour as an ardent proselyte of Mohammed utters praises to his Maker from the housetop at sunrise.

But even this pastime was too tame for the restless nature which constantly pined for the more exciting fun of America. So the chicken stock suddenly declined in value, and that of the swine took a corresponding rise, when there was talk of organizing a

29

football association. This plan, however, lost its popularity after several practices on the "Gridiron"—the climate of Luzon had its drawbacks when it came to punting the pigskin. The requirements for a good football game are a temperature of 6 degrees below zero, and a field covered with a four-inch layer of snow and a corresponding thickness of soft mud underneath. As the Philippines are sadly deficient in the first two articles, it was decided to drop "rugby" in favour of baseball.

Throughout the Eighth Army Corps this proposition was received with great warmth. Every organization had its team. Some influential men of Manila offered inducements to the winning nine; the American Commercial Company agreed to present a silver cup to the team which could score the most points. Arrangements were made for matches, and rival teams soon met on the diamond at the Lunetta. Utah was not to be outdone even in baseball; any man who had ever played ball or looked at a diamond was invited to join the team, and after this liberal request, it took no great time for the battalion to put a pretty good organization into the field. Soon the husky farmers from Utah were pitted against the powerful "pumpkin rollers" from Nebraska, and the sturdy Pennsylvanians fought for honours with the Wyoming cowboys.

Those were pleasant hours when the sons of America met under the tropic sky on a foreign soil and exchanged friendly greeting in their national game. Not a follower of the "Stars and Stripes" was there but felt happier and prouder after such a day. Home seemed nearer by half than it ever had before. And the natives, too, came in for a share of the rejoicing; they liked to see the "Grande Americano" perform his antics with the ball; they, too, gathered in knots and talked and gesticulated and laughed and cheered. The irrepressible small boy was everywhere present, with his sarsaparilla, his peanuts and his slabs of cocoanut candy. There were those who made his trade profitable and those who preferred something of a more fiery nature. That also could be obtained for the asking.

So the games went on by the side of the great swelling sea, and the roll of the surf mingled with the merry tones of the players. Battles were fought and fields were won on the diamond and Utah carried the trophy away to America.

* * * * *

While there were some things which excited the curiosity, others which aroused the attention, and still others which seemed to rivet men's minds for a short time on certain subjects, yet they all paled into insignificance before the magic of that one word *mail!*

On a quiet sultry day, when all nature except the sun seemed to be taking a rest and when nothing but the bugle call for dinner could prove that a spark of life remained in the barracks, the announcement that mail had arrived would transform that peaceful quiet building into an Eastern bazaar, with all of its accessions. At the mention of that word the stolid sentry, pacing his beat with languid steps, instantly quickened into life; the motionless somnolent forms lying on the canvas cots sprang from their recumbent positions, strangely wide awake; the groups of men engaged in a social game of cards, instantly scattered for that new field of interest. The First sergeant's office became a scene of the greatest activity. An eager, excited crowd gathered around; cheeks and noses were pressed against the iron grating, while the ear listened intently for familiar names. Happy was he who received a goodly supply.

"Old guard fatigue" at the Cuartel

There were those who turned away crestfallen and disappointed, there were others who remained behind and hungrily eyed their more fortunate comrades, as they knew they had no loved ones to write to them. When the mail had been distributed the barracks again relapsed into silence, but it was a wide awake silence, not a sultry, oppressive one. Then was reading of letters which told of love and friendship and hope; then were familiar scenes brought before the imagination to renew acquaintances which had begun to grow dim; then were sighs heard for dear home and mother. Newspapers and magazines were not unpopular. The letters read, then the papers were devoured. Long articles, short articles, advertisements and pictures were consumed with equal eagerness, and when every visible portion had been absorbed they were held up to the light to see if they contained anything on the inside. Such was mail day in Manila, and the story proceeds.

In the early days of barrack life, men talked of returning home to celebrate Thanksgiving, but after October had begun to decline it became evident that these fond hopes were not to be realized.

Then the inventive Yankee proceeded to devise means to give thanks in the good old fashioned way in spite of climate and strange country. The Luzon turkey in all respects does not compare favourably with his American cousin, yet he is "turkey," and that goes a great way when it comes to celebrating Thanksgiving.

It was upon this peculiar species of the feathered race that the batterymen fastened their attentions. Turkeys were secured, and they served as a nucleus about which all preparations centred. Several weeks prior to the gala day most elaborate arrangements were made. The soldiers gathered in knots and discussed the coming event. It had a particular interest with them as they anticipated something more palatable than the ordinary "hardtack and slum-gullion." Nor were their expectations disappointed, for, when the day came in all its glory, the commissary had proved itself equal to the occasion. All the powers of the culinary art had been brought to bear upon the leathery tendons of this turkey of the East. It had been fried and flayed until the very air of the barracks became aromatic with its savour. Even the hungry natives scented the perfumed air and gathered at the entrances to inspect the delicacies more closely.

At length the tables were prepared and the ravenous warriors seated themselves. Then were the victuals attacked with vigour; the enemy brought forth all his fighting force; he assaulted the front with deadly effect; simultaneously he attacked the flank and the rear; he cut, he hacked, he slashed, he dissected and tore, until there was nothing left of his victim but the skeleton, and even this he eyed ravenously. Of course there were pies and cakes and cranberries and fruits and greens and vegetables, and they, too, suffered. Of the squash family there were not a few, the favourite pumpkin was wanting, but then the lack of it had been long since supplied by the desiccated potato, and the consumer felt no secret pangs at its absence. Thus Thanksgiving passed on and Christmas came with its bevy of holiday boxes, and its *"Peace on earth good will to men;"* but while the American was still thinking of the light of peace, there came the low rumbling of impending gloom; his ears were startled by the distant thunder of the voice of war; he knew it to be the opening peal of the awakening insurrection and his attention turned to the more serious matter of the imminent conflict. A more powerful enemy than his late foe menaced him from all sides.

Chapter 3

The Insurrection

The report of a rifle rang down the quiet Santa Mesa hill on the night of February 4th. As the flash of the gun died away in the gloom a dusky warrior fell in death and the spark of an insurrection kindled into flame. Almost instantly the belligerent Tagalans rushed down upon the American outposts; the United States forces from Caloocan to Malate swung into line, and the sturdy Anglo-Saxon and the fiery Malay were matched in combat.

The violent clash caused no look of surprise to flutter across the faces of the American soldiers; all knew that the outbreak was coming, all had waited with expectant excitement for the impending conflict. To the intoxicated native victory against the Spanish seemed too certain to be wrested from him by the conquering American; he had long smarted under the goading reflection that "the wreath of the conqueror" had been snatched away at the moment when it seemed almost within his grasp. This bitter knowledge irritated and maddened him, until he only awaited an opportunity to spring at the throat of his imaginary foe and wrench from him what he considered his own. He remembered the long years of wretchedness under Spanish tyranny and oppression. He suspected that his new masters would prove even more overbearing than his late persecutors. He had not forgotten the daring rush for liberty which his ancestors had made. Their blood coursed through his veins and he determined that he would not relinquish the struggle without one last bold dash for the coveted goal.

It was not alone a love for liberty which spurred onward the dark horde which followed the red banner of Aguinaldo. Since 1896 they had striven with their ancient enemy, with the hope that they might tear from him all his wealth. Their leader had with subtle diplomacy urged on his wary braves with the thought that when they battered down the walls of Manila all that it contained would be theirs to loot and ravage. They loved liberty, but they loved the gold which it would bring still more. So they looked with hungry eyes when they saw the Americano enter the city of their dreams and close the gate against the black hosts who sought entrance to plunder and steal.

During the few months preceding the outbreak the Filipinos had become less friendly to their late allies. *La Independencia*, the official organ of the insurgents, frequently came out with loud denunciations against the Americans and called the sullen natives to action against the hated usurpers. It was not an uncommon occurrence to see the walls of public buildings patched over with *proclamos*, signed by Aguinaldo, almost openly declaring war against the Americans and asserting the rights of the Tagalans to their independence.

The fourteen blockhouses which had been the Spanish line of defence had been allowed to fall into the hands of the Filipinos, who converted them into a strong offensive and defensive work. When by chance an American strayed beyond these fortifications, the attitude of the native sentries was often violent and abusive. Eventually no soldiers were permitted to go outside of the territory bounded by our outposts, and the Malay line of muskets tightened around the city like the arm of a colossal dragon. Repeatedly there were war alarms, and for several days the men not on duty were kept in barracks. At times the Tagalans at the pumping station shut off the water supply merely as an insolent challenge and an indication of what they were able to do. On certain parts of the line the Filipinos were seen building new entrenchments and reinforcing the old ones.

For several weeks natives had been concentrating around the Santa Mesa, and Lieutenant Webb was sent out to the Nebraska camp with the left platoon of Battery A to strengthen the Nebraska position. The Santa Mesa road was looked upon by the multitude of Aguinaldo as the natural gateway to Manila. It was at the San Juan Del Monte bridge that they had sought in vain to pound their way into the Spanish lines on many a desperate battle night. One of the Utah guns occupied the very gun pit which had been used by the Castilians as a defence from which their cannon barked back defiance to the onrushing fanatical hordes. Often there were wrangles between Colonel Stotsenberg and the Tagalan officers regarding the line of outposts which the native forces should occupy. Several times the colonel averted hostilities by a judicious yielding to minor points. Ultimately at the San Juan bridge a stalwart American sentry and a diminutive Tagalan paced in parallel lines. The Filipinos seemed anxious to aggravate the Americans into an act of hostility, and rigorous orders were issued to prevent such an occurrence. Night after night the native warriors clustered about one end of the bridge and uttered curses at the silent Nebraskan outpost. Before the outbreak actually took place several times our sentries were forced back by a howling mob of drunken Malays.

One native officer was particularly violent. Not a night passed but that he gathered a crowd of inebriated Tagalans and tramped down to the bridge for the purpose of scoffing and hurling vile epithets at the taciturn American posted there. They were encouraged by the lenient and apparently submissive attitude of the Americans whom they had begun to look upon as arrant cowards, who could be wheedled and whipped about as they chose.

On the night when the signal shot sang out in the darkness and the battle came, the same haughty officer was coming down towards the American line to repeat his abusive conduct, when the sharp voice of the sentry rang out as a warning to halt. He persistently advanced and at the same time launched some vehement Tagalan curses at the outpost. The next instant he lay dead with a bullet through his heart; the report startled the still night air and an insurrection was born.

All that night the thunders of the united American forces in action were wafted to the Cuartel. The natives were so close that some of the bullets pattered against the walls of the building and some even struck the Hotel De Oriente, nearer town. When the commissary wagons probed their way out to the belligerent front they were fired upon from the houses lining the streets. Every *nipa* hut in which a private family lived became an arsenal.

The trouble had been anticipated and every officer knew what portion he was expected to defend. Ten minutes after the news arrived in the Cuartel, the heavy guns of Utah rumbled over the streets to different parts of the field.

Those under Major Grant rushed out into the night and were instantly under a vigorous fire near the woods of Caloocan. Captain Wedgewood disappeared in the blackness and took up the appointed position on the Balic Balic road near Sampaloe cemetery. The guns under Lieutenant Seaman dashed out of the barracks and a few moments later their deep bass was added to the Satanic roar. On McLeod's hill surrounded by the Nebraskans two guns under Lieutenant Webb menaced the plain below.

At Santa Mesa the fight began. Three minutes after the opening flash the Nebraskan camp was deserted. As the outposts slowly returned the regiment swept onward to the fray, and soon the angry rattle of the "Long Toms" answered back the viperous *ping* of the Mauser.

The sound of the first shot had hardly ceased echoing upon the hill when the Tagalans, jubilant, confident, flew for the bridge; their onrush was met with a volley from the Nebraskans. Then from Caloocan and Sampaloe the din of multitudinous musketry fired in unison, waved over the hill; then the awful thunder of the guns of the fleet pulverized the enemy's bulwarks at Malate swelled over the plain. Occasionally a lull came in the fight and then as if gathering strength by inaction the tumult broke forth with increased fury. In the darkness it was impossible for the Utah guns to accomplish anything, as the location of the infantry could not be exactly distinguished. So all night the men tugged and toiled to get the pieces in position, that they might take part in the encounter at dawn. The fifth section gun held a commanding position on the right and the sixth section was stationed directly in front of McLeod's house, from which point it could sweep the enemy's line from Blockhouse No. 7 on the north to the Catholic convent on the south.

Just as the first streaks of dawn dappled the east, the two big guns belched over the plain and the fight began. During the night the relative positions of the opposing forces had not been changed. The maddened Filipinos made a renewed attempt to cross the bridge and penetrate the Nebraska line, that they might gain their coveted goal—the city of their dreams. The aim of the two guns was concentrated upon this point. Twice the Tagalans with frenzied courage charged up the bridge, only to be torn to pieces by the shrieking shells and the deadly bullets. With desperate energy they hauled an artillery piece into position on the bridge, but this was demolished by a single shell from one of our guns.

The position of the artillery became perilous; the insurgents centred a galling fire upon the big guns, with the hope of ridding themselves of this new terror. The leaden missiles rained from three points, Blockhouse No. 7, the bridge and the convent. Every time one of the cannon roared over the hill, she raised a vicious hail of bullets from the enemy. Three minutes after the conflict began Corporal John G. Young received a fatal wound in the lungs. Almost immediately after Private Wilhelm I. Goodman fell dead with a bullet through his brain.

Instantly men rushed in to fill their places, but the position of the gun had become so dangerous that Lieutenant Webb ordered it removed to a more sheltered point, at the north of the house. In the face of a heavy fire the men lifted the piece out of the pit and rolled it to the station designated. This ended the casualty list of the artillery for that day. Both guns now shelled the enemy at Blockhouse No. 7 and the San Juan Del Monte Church, until the two guns under Lieutenant Gibbs came up. The skilled aim of the two gunners and the superb courage of Lieutenant Webb and Sergeants Fisher and Robinson were greatly commended.

Shortly before 11 o'clock two Nordenfelt guns under Lieutenant Gibbs arrived at the hill and under the orders of Colonel Smith of the Tennesseeans advanced up the Santa Mesa road. The Tagalans were still in strong force in the woods to the right of the road, and, as the two guns moved forward, they received a pelting fire from this locality.

The guns dashed up the road and swung into action on the bridge. The forces then began an advance up the road, running twenty and thirty yards at a time, supported by the infantry from Tennessee. After a half hour of sharp fighting the Tagalans fled before the canister and shrapnel of the big guns and the bullets of the Tennesseeans, and thus the hills as far as the Deposito were won. Meanwhile, a battalion of Tennesseeans had deployed out to the left and taken the Deposito, and the two guns were moved to this point.

The Tennesseans left the Nebraskans in charge of the Deposito and disappeared off to the right. Late that night Lieutenant Webb and the fatigued warriors of Santa Mesa joined Lieutenant Gibbs at the Deposito, where they bivouacked with the prospect on the morrow of an advance upon the pumping station, four miles beyond.

The movement upon the pumping station was not easily accomplished; there were several sharp skirmishes on the way. Though the power of the insurgents seemed to have been broken on the previous day, there were some in whom the spirit of resistance was not entirely extinguished and they contested the march of the Americans with vigour. When the move was made on the morning of the 6th the artillery was under the personal command of Major Young. A straggling line of infantry deployed on either side of the road and with the artillery in the rear the forward movement began. Scarcely half a mile from the Deposito the moving column encountered a small body of Tagalans, who opened fire. Once more the angry guns pealed forth in menacing thunder and the terror-stricken natives retreated for the kind shelter of the bamboo thickets beyond. Two similar skirmishes happened farther up the road. About a mile and a half from the Deposito the mutilated body of Dr. Harry A. Young was found lying by the side of a ventilator. Some distance back the body of his horse had been discovered. Major Young was the first to locate this gory evidence, which mutely told the tragic story of the end of Dr. Young. All the clothing had been rent from the body, a bullet hole was in his forehead, and a bolo wound from the elbow of the left arm to the waist told the tragic story of how he died. The supposition is that the Doctor was surprised on his way to the Deposito, where he had an appointment with Major Young, and took the wrong road, which led him to a grim death in the Tagalan territory. A few minutes later, while the body was being conveyed to Manila, the major calmly commanded his men in a rush with the enemy, in which eighty of them were killed. This exhibition of splendid courage was ever after an inspiration to the Utahn when he felt like being disheartened.

Gradually the uncoiled infantry line pushed back the recalcitrant natives, and late in the morning the heights above the beautiful Mariquina valley were reached. Here the artillery was placed in position, and, with the Mariquina Church steeple as a target, the town was bombarded. Now and then a shuddering shrapnel was sent shrieking after fugitive bands of Tagalans, who made all haste for the protecting shelter of the mountain on the opposite side of the valley.

From that place they were content to look with dismay upon the death-dealing monsters which frowned from the hill above the bulwarks.

When the first platoon of Battery A, under Captain Wedgewood, sped out into the gloom on the night of the 4th it took up a position in the Balic Balic road near the Cemetario de Sampaloe. All night long the two guns were under a straggling fire from the Filipinos, who at this place held Blockhouse No. 5, about 300 yards to our front, and a diminutive stone church which was located off to the right of our position. The section two gun was placed inside the Cemetario, but that of section one remained outside, where it was exposed to the enemy's fire.

At 3 a.m. from two points the Malays centred a vicious fusillade upon the artillery, which remained inactive owing to the obscurity of the Tagalan line of defence. No. 1 gun was moved back about 100 yards to a more sheltered station by the cemetery. Just as the first streaks of dawn appeared in the east the two guns blazed toward the blockhouse and the small church, in which were a large number of natives. Simultaneously the Colorado infantry swung into position and with a withering fire slowly advanced upon the enemy. Several well-directed shells sent the Filipinos flying from the blockhouse and a few more accurately trained shots annihilated the little church. As the Tagalans moved from their cover they fell many deep before the blasting volleys of the invincible Coloradoans.

As the natives fled from the church, the artillery turned its attention to Blockhouse No. 4, 1700 yards distant, and while the South Dakotans made a wonderful charge they demolished this wooden bulwark. Next the big guns were ordered to shatter Blockhouse No. 6, but before they could be brought into play against this point the insurgents had disappeared into the woods with the swift-moving Colorado infantrymen hard on their track. On the 6th the platoon was moved to a position left of Blockhouse No. 7. On this part of the line it remained until March 23rd, when it was ordered to Caloocan to take part in the fierce engagement at that point when the whole line charged the enemy's works on March 25th.

The damage inflicted on the natives of Sampaloe was very considerable. Over a hundred bodies were buried there and in many a battered form could be seen that ripping course of a shrapnel. General Hale personally praised the work of Sergeants Emil Johnson and W. E. Kneass, who were in immediate charge of the two rifles.

The guns of Battery B took a position on the left of the line to the south of Caloocan on the night of the war alarm. Second Lieutenant Seaman went out on the Caloocan road with one 3.2 gun. Major Grant left the Cuartel with three 3.2-inch guns, and after leaving one at Bilibid Prison took the remaining two up the rugged Bulum Bugan road as far as Lazaro Hospital. Emplacements were made under a spattering fire from the enemy at this point, facing the Chinese Hospital and the Binondo Cemetery, in both of which places the Tagalans were strongly lodged. Only an occasional shot blazed towards the enemy during the night, but from a commanding position the artillery fire began at dawn with destructive and terrifying results. Besides driving the sturdily-entrenched Tagalans back, the Utah attack entirely covered the simultaneous advance of the Tenth Pennsylvania and South Dakota infantry.

The advance of the slowly-moving regiment was irresistible and the natives fell back from their position after a stubborn fight. All that day the Malay resisted the American advance with fanatical frenzy. The artillery moved forward at the same moment, but many times was delayed by burning huts. After an advance of about 400 yards they again joined the infantry line, but they had arrived at a conspicuous and dangerous position on the road, where for thirty minutes they fought desperately in the open under a heavy fire from the Filipino entrenchments. It was here that Major Bell of General McArthur's staff rode up and requested Major Grant to move up beyond the Chinese Hospital, where the Tagalans in a fierce engagement were inflicting heavy damage on the infantry. Almost at the same moment Colonel Wallace sent word that a company of the Tenth Pennsylvanians had been cut off to the left, and Lieutenant Critchlow was sent with one gun up the Leco road to its assistance. The remaining guns tore the woods in front of the advancing infantry and cleared the way for the Pennsylvanians and South Dakotans, so that the right wing advanced at this point almost without a casualty. Still towards Caloocan the artillery advanced with the musketeers, and beyond the Cemetery Church the big guns shelled the woods to the left of La Loma in front of the advancing Third United States Artillery (infantry) and Twentieth Kansas. Just when the Tagalans were fleeing, bleak with terror, from the artillery shells; when Colonel Funston, like a young Jove, was pounding his way irresistibly up from the left, and when everything looked auspicious for an easy dash into Caloocan, word came from General MacArthur that the firing should cease. The spires of Caloocan were then almost in view, and there is an opinion that had General MacArthur not feared that the line would grow too thin by a further advance Funston would have taken Caloocan that night, with many railway cars and many supplies, and with the saving of many lives which went out on the next advance when the Filipinos had had time to bulwark themselves behind their wonderful entrenchments.

On the same day the guns were moved to a position close to La Loma Church. Later two Nordenfelt guns arrived, one of Battery A, and were stationed first at Blockhouse No. 3 and afterwards east of La Loma Church and in front of the left battalion of the South Dakota infantry. These were commanded by Lieutenant Critchlow.

Meanwhile Lieutenant Seaman withstood a destructive fire on the Caloocan road. Early in the fight he was reinforced at the suggestion of the division commander by the addition of another gun. Major Young took personal command of the Nordenfelt which arrived there late that night. Frequently in the encounter the natives rushed up to within 150 yards of our position, from which they went reeling back before the awful thunder of the big guns. At times the powder-begrimed Utahns were in advance of the main line, carrying death into the very teeth of the foe. So fierce was the conflict that Major Young had the gun manipulated in short reliefs, and this shortened the casualty list of our organization. Corporal Wardlaw and Private Peter Anderson sustained wounds while serving their pieces in this manner. The natives trained two big guns on our position and fired fifteen ineffective shots from them. Next day the two guns supported the Kansas troops in their advance upon the Filipino entrenchments and Blockhouse No. 1. As the swift-moving column charged the enemy's line the two rifles tore great gaps into this wooden structure and ploughed furrows into the wonderfully-constructed earthworks. When the insurgents had fled before the deadly volleys of the Kansans one gun was stationed at the blockhouse and the other at the Binondo Cemetery. Here they remained until February 10th, when they took part in the demonstration against Caloocan.

The next three days Major Grant's three guns did nothing except to fire occasionally at some enthusiastic Filipino sharpshooters. On the 11th a general advance was made by the Montana and the Kansas infantry and the Third United States Artillery. The artillery force consisted of two guns under Lieutenant Seaman on the hill to the left, two guns under Lieutenant Fleming of the Sixth United States Artillery on the railroad, Lieutenant Critchlow with two Nordenfelts at Blockhouse No. 2, and Grant with three 3.2-inch B. and L. rifles at La Loma Church. The prearranged signal for the attack was to be a bombardment by the navy accompanied by a similar action by Major Young's artillery force. The big guns pounded shell against the native defences, and sent shrapnel singing into the woods surrounding the town, and under the somewhat ineffectual, but loudly-thundering labours of the fleet the infantry column hurried forward, and the Tagalans gradually swayed back. As the enemy retreated the aim of the guns was directed higher and several of these iron messengers went crashing into the town. Some remarkably good work was performed by our gunners on this day. It is said that a small body of Filipinos could be seen reinforcing the entrenchments at the gate of the Caloocan Cemetery. A Utah gunner saw this, and turned his piece on the gate and shortly after a shell shuddered through the air on its 2600-yard journey. When the smoke cleared away, gate, Filipinos and war weapons strewed the ground for many yards.

Major Bell with a flanking column of Montanas deployed through a ravine on the right. Suddenly a long, rope-like column of natives whipped out of the fringe of the woods and quickly coiled around the company. Major Young saw the predicament in which the Americans were placed, and soon the murderous shells fell in the midst of the column, which broke into fragments and disappeared the way it had come. The next day Major Bell was lavish in his praise of the batteries, and several British officers who were watching the progress of the fight complimented the gunners on their expert and effective gunnery.

During the attack on Caloocan Lieutenant Seaman followed with the infantry as far as the flames from the burning houses would permit and pulled the gun through Caloocan to a position on the Kansas line. On the 11th guns were moved to a position on a hillside near the residence of Mr. Higgins near Caloocan at a place where he commanded the causeway between Caloocan and Malabon. At this point the two guns were joined by a platoon of the Sixth Artillery and a 3.6 mortar under Corporal Boshard of Battery B.

LIEUT. GIBBS' SECTION AT FT. MACARTHUR

At this time Utah soldiers on different parts of the line manned thirty-two pieces of artillery, including 3.2-inch B.L. rifles, Hotchkiss revolving cannon, Hotchkiss mountain guns, Maxim Nordenfelts captured from the Spanish, Mortars, Colt's rapid-fire (Browning's) gun, a navy field piece, navy six-pounder and Gatling guns of various calibres.

After Caloocan was taken possession of by the troops scarcely any fighting was indulged in until March 25th, when an advance was made. Except for occasional incursions into the enemy's territory for the purpose of driving back harassing sharpshooters there was a practical cessation of hostilities at the waterworks. At this time the line over which our guns were stationed extended from Malabon to Mariquina. At Caloocan a severe engagement occurred on the 23rd of February. A large force of insurgents came rushing down from the hill towards our outposts and finally established themselves within 150 yards of the American lines. It was during this period that some of them were able to penetrate the American position and steal their way into Manila to take part in the burning of the Tondo district. This band was under the leadership of a bold and gallant chief named Zandico. While Tondo was disappearing in flames and sharp hand-to-hand skirmishes were taking place between these Filipino desperadoes and the American police a furious altercation was going on between the darkly-outlined bulwarks of the two armies. During this attack sixty men of the Kansas and Montana regiments alone were killed and wounded.

The work of the sharpshooters showed the watchful alertness of the enemy. Whenever one of these riflemen espied a piece of American anatomy there was a report and a still messenger of death went skimming through the air. Frequently one of the large guns had to be employed to repress the zeal of one of these ubiquitous Malays. While repairing a breach in the gun pit Lieutenant Seaman received a wound in the leg, Corporal Southers was shot in the hip and Private Hill sustained a serious wound in the back.

About this time existed as remarkable a truce as was ever patched up between belligerent forces. Some Filipino statesmen came down from Malabon to see Aguinaldo, and as they carried a flag of truce firing from our side ceased. The natives signified their desire to talk and Colonel Funston and Major Young went half way to meet them. The Tagalans then made known their proposition, which was that there should be no firing between the two forces at that point for a period of ten days. Colonel Funston assented. This was directly in front of the Kansas line. The insurgents rigidly adhered to their promise, and while the Springfields and Mausers were angrily barking in the vicinity of the railroad track no messenger of war sped across the space in front of the Kansans.

*   *   *   *   *

The four guns under Lieutenant Gibbs and Webb lifted to a commanding position on the hill above the waterworks, menaced the valley below. Frequently they boomed from the mountains as a warning to the curious natives down on the wide plain of the San Mateo. The encounters which took place between the Americans and the Tagals at this place are illustrative of the peculiar mode of warfare carried on by the natives. Not a few times our forces made invasions in the enemy's country at Mariquina under the protection of the guns and drove his army into the foothills on the opposite side of the valley, only to find him back in his old position before nightfall with his camp fires piercing the gloom of the valley as darkness settled in.

These successive defeats seemed to have no power in dampening the ardour of the ducky warriors of the plains. They continued to make invasions on the American territory, and frequently waylaid belated American troops. Up to March 25th the infantry force was not sufficiently large to hold the country which had been taken. Four times the town of Mariquina was captured in this style. Finally, by some peculiar decision of fate, a battalion of Coloradoans descended into the valley and after dislodging the enemy set fire to the hideous *nipa* huts. Thereafter fewer skirmishes occurred in this locality. The white and shining church steeple arose above the blackened ruins as a ghostly monument of the work of war.

About four days after the occupancy of the waterworks by the American troops Colonel Stotsenberg with a small body of the infantry scoured the Mariquina plain, but though he met with some heated skirmishes and drove the enemy back, there was no visible results from his excursion. The artillery was first used in an advance on February 17th, when the two Nordenfelt guns were taken down the Mariquina road by Lieutenant Gibbs. None of the Utah men were hurt on this occasion, although the natives fought stubbornly at short range and several men and officers of the Nebraska regiment were wounded. Meanwhile General Montenegro, known as one of the fiercest Filipino chiefs, had congregated his forces in the woods southwest of the pumping station towards Pasig Lake and Cainta. A plan was formed for surrounding the insurgents and the Nebraska and Washington infantry and the two Maxim Nordenfelts took part in the engagement. The artillery worked with the Nebraskans and shelled the woods. Then there was a simultaneous advance from two sides by the regiments. The Washingtons did their work well and the shells from the guns were effective, but for once the Nebraskans failed in their usual dash and came up too late to cut off the retreat of the enemy and prevent his escape.

GUN AT PUMPING STATION FIRING ON MARIQUINA

Again on the 24th the two Nordenfelts under Lieutenant Webb moved down the Mariquina road, and did excellent work in aiding the Nebraskans to drive the natives back towards San Mateo. The B. and L. rifles from the hill fired into bodies of natives to the left of Mariquina Church on this occasion, and the death roster of the insurgents for that day was very great. A revolving Hotchkiss under Corporal Hesburg, located close to the Deposito, also inflicted severe damage on the natives. Still the enemy at this point was alert and aggressive. The next day Major Mulford went scouting with a small force to the right of Mariquina. Soon after he reached the valley he was completely surrounded by the insurgents. Then the big guns on the hill sent bursting shells fast into the Filipino ranks and soon they retired stubbornly into the woods. Several of Major Mulford's men were killed or wounded, and he stated afterwards that the Utah guns had saved himself and party. This skirmish proved that the natives were gathering there in a larger and more formidable force, and this circumstances led to the burning of Mariquina. All night the flames from the bamboo huts and old Spanish mansions illumined the valley, and when the troops descended the next morning they found that all the south and the greater part of the north end of the city were entirely destroyed.

There was comparative quietude after that until March 6th, when the natives began to resume the annoying fire on the infantry, and an artillery demonstration became imperative. As the insurgent attack came about daylight, the guns under Lieutenant Gibbs bombarded the valley from the hill, driving the enemy northward. Another large force of the Tagalans swept down upon the Nebraskan outposts on the left and a deadly affray commenced. Reinforcements were rushed to the aid of the stricken sentries, who were gradually forced back by the superior numbers of the assaulting party. Sergeant Ford Fisher with the fifth section gun dashed out of the camp to the front. For three-quarters of a mile the diminutive Filipinos horses with which the guns had lately been equipped sped down the ridges under a galling fire. On the brow of the hill the gun whirled into action long enough to drive the enemy back a few hundred yards. Again the piece limbered up and rattled over the hard lava road for a new position. The Tagalans soon centred a murderous fire from three points upon the big gun as a desperate measure to annihilate this new terror. A horse ridden by Private Engler was shot down, but was able to recover himself sufficiently to gain the shelter of a small gulch a few yards farther on. From its shelter the big gun pounded over the road to another gulch which had been deserted just a few minutes previously by a company of Nebraskans. The heavy limber chest was left at the foot of the hill and on their hands and knees the men pushed the piece forward until the bore of the gun gleamed down the slope. A heavy volley answered from the plain below. Ford Fisher said afterwards that he saw a Filipino sharpshooter behind a rock fire six times point blank at the gunner as he was sighting the piece. Suddenly the roar of a cannon tore down the hill. The Tagalans answered it with a fiendish yell and came steadily onward. The men on the gun worked like Trojans, but they could not force the Malays back. Just as it seemed as if the gun would have to retire the tall white figure of Colonel

Stotsenberg could be seen with galloping steed coming up the hill. Instantly the wavering infantry line tightened. The colonel's pistol flashed in the sunlight, and the whole column swung up the eminence to victory. The voice of the big gun bellowed back its notes of defiance and the haughty foe fled in terror.

During the encounter Corporal McDonald with a revolving Hotchkiss cannon performed some excellent service on the right in aiding the Oregon infantry. Most of the fighting had been done at from 100 to 150 yards range. The casualty list of the Nebraskans was heavy, and an immense number of Filipinos was killed. The infantry followed the retreating natives for three miles.

On the 7th, in conjunction with the river fleet, the guns aided the Nebraska, Wyoming and Washington infantry in forcing the enemy through the woods towards Guadaloupe and Pasig Lake. The guns under Captain Wedgewood shelled the insurgents to the south of San Juan del Monte and aided the infantry very materially in its advance. The gunboats hammered the natives on the left bank of the river and sent them scurrying into the woods beyond Guadaloupe.

It was decided to take the town of Mariquina on the 16th of March, and Major Young with the left platoon of Battery A shelled the woods to the north and west of the town so effectively that when the infantry forces entered the place they found it deserted.

UTAH GUNS ON MANILA & DAGUPAN RAILWAY *EN ROUTE* FOR THE FRONT

This ended the fighting in that vicinity until the general advance of March 25th.

On March 25th began that remarkable advance which never ended until the native forces were driven beyond Calumpit and San Fernando into the hills north of San Isidro and Tarlac. The American forces had long been inactive gathering strength for the difficulties before them, and now that this strength had been mustered they were eager for the fray. The plan was for the commands of Generals H. G. Otis and Hale to swing around to the right and cut off the retreat of the enemy from that quarter, while General Wheaton's brigade was to strike the foe in front and not move forward until the other forces had had sufficient time to straighten out the line. A large body of the insurgents had assembled at Malabon. The entire preparation had been made for the capture of this force.

Otis's brigade on the left consisted in the order given of the Kansas, the Third Artillery (infantry), and the Montana regiment; in the centre was the divisional artillery under Major Young and then troops of the Fourth United States Cavalry, and on the right was Hale's command, containing the Tenth Pennsylvania, South Dakota and Nebraska regiments. The Nebraskans were on the extreme right, while the Kansans formed the pivotal regiment.

The artillery designated to take part in the forward movement were two B. and L. rifles, under command of Lieutenant Critchlow; two B.L. rifles of the Sixth United States Artillery, under Lieutenant Fleming, and an automatic gun under command of Ensign Davis of the navy. On the evening of the 24th Lieutenant Fleming's guns were removed from the old entrenchment in front of Fort MacArthur, and were replaced by two B. and L. rifles under Lieutenant Gibbs of Battery A, who had formerly been stationed in front of the Colorado line at Sampaloe. Major Grant at this period was no longer in immediate command of Battery B, as he had been detailed as commander of the river gunboats on February 17th. During the period of waiting the Government mules had arrived and the rifles under Lieutenants Critchlow and Fleming were now equipped for the journey into the jungle.

Few artillery exploits can compare in dash and daring with that performed by Lieutenant Naylor out on the right of the line early in the morning of the 25th. Many brave and reckless deeds with guns at close range were done by artillery forces on other occasions in the Filipino campaign, but it is hardly probable that any field pieces have been rushed so far beyond infantry support as they were on this day before the enemy at San Francisco del Monte.

Lieutenant Naylor's position lay in a sunken road at a point where the lines of the Tenth Pennsylvania and South Dakota regiments joined. For a distance of about 800 yards the road, which had been constructed by the Spanish, extended toward the Tagalan earthworks. At the point the road abruptly ends, and there is a plat of hard ground. Fifty yards farther on a rude barricade had been erected as a shelter for the native outposts, and a hundred yards in advance of this the enemy's strong line of earthworks widened out across the top of a gently rising eminence. This position had been accurately located several days previously by a reconnoitring party. Early in the morning the guns moved to the end of the sunken road and began the perilous journey up this narrow defile. With Lieutenant Naylor were Captain Crainbuhl and Lieutenant Perry of General Hale's staff and a detachment of eight men of the Tenth Pennsylvania Regiment under charge of a sergeant. Every one knew the danger that accompanied an expedition of this character, and there was silence as perfect as that of a tomb, save when one of the wheels of the heavy guns rumbled in a rut. A few hundred yards from the camp they crossed a small stream and, as the road broadened at this place, there was ample room to unlimber the pieces. This was done so that there would be no delay when the time for action should come. The pieces were placed in front and the two limbers followed. At the end of the road the squad of infantry deployed as skirmishers to drive back the Filipino sentries. Then the guns were rushed up on the flat; two shells shrieked through the air towards the insurgent entrenchments, which loomed up darkly on the hill, and the bombardment began. At the first bark of the big guns the native outposts fled precipitately for the protection of the heavier works on the summit of the knoll. The roaring monsters now hurled a perfect stream of iron into the place, and after responding feebly for a few minutes the foe retired in haste across the San Juan River towards San Francisco del Monte. The artillery advanced to the stream and sent shells flying after them until it became too hazardous to continue the bombardment, owing to the approach of our troops. Down the causeway over which the Tagalans fled in their mad desire to escape whole squads of Filipinos lay. As the guns had made the advance almost entirely unaided by the infantry it was purely an artillery charge, and to the artillery belonged the victory. General Hale rode up a few minutes later and personally complimented Lieutenant Naylor upon the ability with which he had handled his men in this successful manoeuvre.

As the guns were unprovided with mules they were unable to proceed and retired to their former position.

The engagement opened up by Lieutenant Naylor's men on the right found an echoing response from the guns of Lieutenants Critchlow and Fleming. As they were to continue the advance their general course lay along the railroad track, which stretches entirely across Luzon Island from Manila to Dagupan. Just after dawn on the 25th the infantry moved forward about 700 yards ahead of the artillery, which followed the Novaliches road. A strong force of the enemy was encountered heavily entrenched in a position commanding the Novaliches and Malinta roads. The infantry swung into line and attempted to force back the Tagalans, who stubbornly resisted the attack of our column. Two large guns were soon brought into play and the natives gradually retired. An examination later showed that the defences of the insurgents were remarkably constructed; in some cases the main breastworks were twenty feet thick. The first day's fighting had taught them a lesson by which they had profited.

General MacArthur gave orders for the artillery to remain with him during the advance, as it was impossible to move over the ridges. A troop of the Fourth Cavalry, under Major Rucker, also remained with the general. In the afternoon the artillery had turned down a small valley toward the bed of the Pulilan River. The infantry had entirely disappeared from the division commander's view, owing to a mountain which lay between our forces and the artillery position. The general whereabouts of our troops could be ascertained by the battle-sound, but occasionally this died away as the moving column advanced. The general sent forward one of his aids with a view of re-establishing our lines; but he was fired upon and compelled to retire. The troops of cavalry then dismounted and deploying as skirmishers soon dislodged the enemy. Soon heavy firing was heard and an orderly rushed back asking for reinforcements. The general sent word back that he had no reinforcements to give. Just then Major Bell rode up and said he wished one of the Utah guns and the general authorized Major Young to take one of the big rifles and a Browning gun under Ensign Davis.

Majors Bell and Young went forward to locate a position for the pieces. They discovered that where the road crosses the river the banks of the Pulilan rise to an almost perpendicular height of nearly fifteen feet. A road a little distance above, so small that it could only be utilized for *carometas*, crosses the river a short distance beyond the dismantled bridge. On the right abutment of the bridge the Filipinos had constructed a very formidable breastwork of earth and stone, and the heavy steel beam of the bridge was arranged above this so as to leave a long slot for the rifles the whole length of the work. This menaced the surrounding approaches. A short distance below this was a boiler and engine-house and on the other side of the river and lower down was a remarkable field work. It extended along the river a distance of two hundred feet, and was constructed with the same wonderful skill as the smaller one at the bridge abutment. It had the same long slot flaring outward about eighteen inches and the upper part of the work was substantially held by bamboo flooring.

The two majors left the artillery piece and went forward to discover a good site for the big gun. Major Young selected a place just under the brow of the hill. The enemy was only 100 yards beyond, but our exact location was screened from his view by a thick undergrowth of bamboo. A heavy stone wall was used as a shelter for the men. Meanwhile the cavalry stood a terrific fire. Out of less than forty men who took part in the encounter nine were killed and wounded, a casualty list of almost one-fourth of their number. The guns rushed into action. Major Young directed that the Colt's automatic be turned on the slots to protect the big gun. At the first boom of the rifle all the attention of the insurgents was turned upon the crews working the piece, but the bamboo screen kept them from taking accurate aim. Of the three shells fired by Corporal Don Johnson, two struck immediately in the slot holes and burst in the interior, doing considerable damage to the bamboo shed and above all terrifying the dusky warriors, who turned and fled. The spitting Colts and breaking shrapnel followed them with deadly effect. The artillery then lumbered up and dashed to a position on the hill, from which the boiler-house could be bombarded with annihilating effect. The cavalry had stood a heavy fire during all this time at a range of seventy-five yards, and when the beam had been examined after the enemy had been driven out it showed the marks of eighty-nine cavalry bullets.

That night the weary troops rested on the banks of the river. The next morning, March 26th, an early advance was made upon the insurgents' position at Malinta and Polo. It was here the moving column met the advancing lines of General Wheaton, and then it was learned that he had marched forward simultaneously with Hale's flying command, and that the wily native had had ample time to flee out of Malabon and his old position at Caloocan. So the projected coup had failed. Lieutenant Gibbs with the right platoon of Battery A and one gun of Battery B and a mortar bombarded Malabon and the surrounding country. When the shelling ceased the Oregon regiment charged over the open and assaulted the enemy's works, which were taken after a stubborn fight. The routed Tagalans fled along the railroad track towards Malinta.

One gun under Lieutenant Seaman accompanied Wheaton on this march as far as the foot of the hill leading to Malinta, and was unloaded from the car under a shower of Mauser bullets. Private Parker J. Hall of Battery B was wounded at this point while standing on the track. A few shells were fired into distant entrenched position on the hill, but when Wheaton resumed his advance early in the morning the B. and L. rifle was returned to its position at Fort MacArthur. It was during the advance up the hill a few moments later that the gallant, white-haired General Egbert, veteran of many battles, was fatally shot through the stomach.

In the meantime the artillery with General MacArthur's division continued the march up the road close by the railway line. While the artillery was sending shell fast into the Filipino position at Malinta and Meycayauan, and occupying their attention, General Hale executed a rather brilliant flank movement and forced the enemy to retreat with considerable loss. When the march was resumed on the 27th, the artillery was moved up to a position just behind the first battalion of the Kansas regiment, while all the rest of Otis's brigade remained in the rear.

FIRST PLATOON. BATTERY A, READY TO MOVE TO MALOLOS

When General MacArthur's division moved forward on March 25th, General Hall, with the Colorado and Minnesota regiments, moved down the Mariquina valley towards the San Francisco del Monte, where the bullets of the South Dakotas and Lieutenant Naylor's shells were battering against the walls. General Hall's advance was so warmly contested that it became necessary for the guns on the hill to bombard the city and surrounding woods to the north and west. The infantry was then able to press forward and drive the natives back from the valley toward San Mateo.

On the 31st of March General Hall essayed a more extended advance, and on this occasion his forces consisted of the Fourth and Twenty-third regular infantry, the Minnesota and Colorado regiments and two Utah B. and L. rifles, commanded by Captain Wedgewood. The movement began at dawn. The regulars came from the South and the Minnesotas and Coloradoans around the north of Mariquina. The town was entered before the enemy had begun to fire. The attack was sudden and effective, and as the natives began to retreat a gun under Sergeant Nystrom and another close by the Mariquina Church commanded by Captain Wedgewood played vigorously on their ranks. The infantry followed the natives six miles, and from the hills overlooking the city San Mateo was bombarded by the two guns.

The natives were again in retreat when a telegram arrived from Otis, which showed that he feared the natives might be preparing to make another entrance into Manila. It read:

> Wheaton has engaged enemy at Malolos and taken that place. A very small force of the enemy was there. Withdraw all your forces which are moving towards San Mateo and bring them back to La Loma Church.

It was a wearisome march to La Loma after the fatigue of the day's campaign, and when the men arrived there with the guns they were forced to sleep among the graves of the churchyard without blankets and in a pelting rain. The next day the guns were ordered back to their old position above Mariquina, where they remained until relieved by the Sixth United States Infantry, when they joined the rest of the command at San Fernando.

On April 27th our forces met the Filipinos on the banks of the Marilao River, on which occasion the noses of the big guns were pushed to within fifty yards of the native earthworks. The guns employed were two under Lieutenant Critchlow, a platoon of Dyer's light battery and Colt's automatic under Ensign Davis. The Kansans under Major Metcalf had deployed on the left and approached the river, but they were forced back by the heavy fire of the insurgents, who had cut away the intervening trees to give a clear sweep for their rifles. The whole north side of the river had been cleverly and completely entrenched so that it formed an almost impregnable fortification when attacked from the front. The causeway up which the artillery had to advance was commanded by the insurgent infantry. Across the river where the infantry first engaged the enemy, the natives were about 800 yards distant. Major Young went forward with Ensign Davis to locate a good position for the guns. While there General Funston came up and stated he had seen quite a number of *cascos* further down the river, and that if Major Young would protect his men with an artillery fire he would be able to cross the river and flank the enemy. This was agreed to, and a company of Kansans accompanied the guns as a support. Lieutenant Critchlow's guns were quickly turned upon the earthworks. As the big rifles roared across the stream the small arms and the Colt's automatic centred a withering fire on the entrenchments to keep the enemy's fire inaccurate. This vigorous demonstration terrified the Tagalans and soon several white flags appeared fluttering above the trenches. The firing ceased and the Filipinos were ordered to stand up. Some few of them reluctantly showed themselves, but the greater number ran through the get-away ditch and vanished in the dark fringe of the bamboo forest. Lieutenant Coulter of the Tenth Pennsylvania regiment with an enlisted man stripped and swam the river and walked directly into the enemy's trenches. The two naked men took as many rifles as they could hold from the defeated Malays. By this time Colonel Funston, who had crossed the river, came up and took some thirty natives prisoners.

As the bridge crossing a branch of the Marilao River at this point had been destroyed by the insurgents, the artillery moved to a new position by the railroad track until a new bridge could be constructed by the engineers. Just as night came on the natives were seen to emerge in a large force from the woods and move towards our lines. Soon the entire American host was sturdily engaged in repelling the attack. In the dark it was impossible to exactly locate our infantry, but Major Young, at a venture, directed several shots over our column at a range of from 2000 to 2500 yards. The Filipinos soon retreated. It was afterwards learned that these shells had fallen in the midst of the attacking force.

This spirited encounter was the subject of a special report of the chief of artillery to the division commander in which Lieutenant Critchlow and the cannoneers received special mention for their gallantry.

That night a pontoon bridge was built across the river and on the morning of the 28th the artillery moved across and encamped during the succeeding day and night in the suburbs of Malolos. An advance of only a short distance had been made the next morning when a body of the enemy was encountered at Bocaue. Here it was necessary to cross the Santa Mone River. This was attempted with some difficulty, as only the guns could be taken over on the bridge and the mules had to be swum across. The pieces and accoutrements across, the artillery immediately went into action against the long lines of Filipinos. A railroad train in the hands of the insurgents could be seen in the distance and some natives were busily engaged in applying torches to the engine-house. A few shells were sent screaming in that direction and the engineer needed no further orders to speed with all dispatch toward the north country. Again the guns were limbered up and the force advanced to the Bagoa River, where it was again necessary to drag the guns across the shaky bridge and force the reluctant mules to swim.

By this time the infantry had pushed some distance ahead, and suddenly there was heavy firing near another dismantled bridge close to the Guiguinta. Both the town and the bridge had been burned by the insurgents, and as soon as the infantry force crossed the railway track it was greeted with such a heavy fire that there were thirty casualties within a few minutes. The artillery came forward, as it had done before in many desperate fights, at the critical moment. The mules were unhitched and the cannoneers dashed with two of the guns across the shattered bridge and began firing from the top of the track. The insurgent fire came directly down the railroad grade. Private Pender was shot through the hip while working at the gun. In a few moments the shrapnel had torn the Filipino earthworks and in the semi-darkness the dusky figures of the Filipinos could be seen in retreat. The river which barred the way was crossed the next day.

When evening fell on the 30th, the towers of Malolos, the insurgent capital, where a few months before Don Emilio Aguinaldo had been crowned president of the Filipino republic, were almost within view. A long line of Filipino entrenchments defended the approaches to the city. All eyes had been turned from the beginning of the insurrection toward Malolos, and here it was expected that on the morrow Aguinaldo, with a host of his black warriors around him, would make a desperate effort to resist the aggression of the American troops. The four big rifles and the Colt's automatic were moved into a position at dusk close to a deserted line of entrenchments south of Malolos. Majors Bell and Young, later in the evening, went forward to locate a position for constructing emplacements for the guns. Suddenly there was a long flash from a low line of Filipino entrenchments 1000 yards to the front. They saw the flash in time to guard themselves by the shelter of a rice stack from the pattering bullets. Their mission by this time was accomplished, for they had discovered a strong position for the rifles just within a circle of bamboo trees from which there was an easy view of the enemy's works.

Late that night, in the tropic darkness of the overhanging trees, a line of men, carrying picks and spades, trudged out slowly from the encampment. They were guided by First Sergeant John Anderson of Battery B. Soon the rice stack where the emplacements were to be made could be seen through the gloom. The work was begun quietly, for the Filipinos in the distance were known to be on the alert. An axe struck sharply against a bamboo and a pick dinned resoundingly in the hard earth. Every one looked searchingly into the distance, where a response was looked for from a hundred guns. Major Young stated that he had posted a lookout near by so that when he called "flash" the men could take care of themselves as they saw fit before the winged bullets arrived. So the work went on. When the earth had been reared about one foot, the lookout suddenly called "flash" and twenty men dropped to the ground. But there was no report and no bullets came. The lookout had seen some restless Filipino lighting a cigarette. The entrenchments were ready shortly after midnight, and before dawn on the morning of the 31st the guns were moved into position. The insurgents formed a belligerent half-circle around the city, and were prepared to advance from three sides when the roar of one of the big guns gave the signal to move. When the light came it brought into bright relief the heavy earthworks of the enemy, and a body of soldiers was observed standing idly on the railroad track about ten hundred yards away. Suddenly the yawning big guns roared over the plain and a shell burst over the Filipino entrenchments. There was a brief response. The vigorous click-click of the automatic joined in with the roar of the big guns. Within an hour the infantrymen were advancing upon the outer works of the city from three sides, and the Filipinos could be seen fleeing down the railroad grade. They were followed by bullets from rapid-fire guns and several shells were sent into the insurgents city at a range of four kilometres. Afterwards it was learned that the natives had been driven from their two lines of entrenchments, which were 1000 yards apart, a fact which clearly indicated the accuracy of the firing. As soon as the enemy was dispersed the pieces were limbered and while one section took the winding course of the Malolos road into the city the other went by way of the railroad. For several thousands yards in front of Malolos the track had been torn up by the insurgents and the gun which went up the track had great difficulty in passing. At one place where the bridge had been destroyed it was necessary to replace a large number of ties which had been hurriedly thrown into a body of water near by.

All morning a long curling line of smoke could be seen from the distance arising from the heart of the city. When the artillery swept into the city side by side with the rigid column of infantry they found half the place in ruins; the great church which had been used as a congressional hall was fading in the flame. The American had found the city a burning Moscow and the people, like the patriotic Russians, had applied the torch to the capital upon which they had centred their fondest dreams. The soldiers trooped into city, mud-bespattered and weary, and commented in loud tones of surprise on their peaceful entry into a city where they had looked for the bloodiest strife of the insurrection. The artillery made a striking appearance as the big mules galloped over the evacuated town. The guns were parked in the plaza before the Hall of Congress of the

UTAH GUNS IN PARK, AT CONGRESSIONAL HALL, MALOLOS

insurgent capital, and Major MacArthur accorded to Major Young the honour of raising the first American flag over the walls of the rebel capital. It may be added here that several weeks later the Utah band played patriotic airs in the hall where but a short time ago Aguinaldo was declared president of the Philippines.

The troops remained for several days inactive at Malolos to recuperate after the rigors of the long march. During this time the two guns commanded by Lieutenant Gibbs at Caloocan were brought to Malolos by rail, and Captain Wedgewood took charge of them, while Lieutenant Gibbs returned to the two platoons stationed at the waterworks.

On April 7th a reconnoitring expedition went out to investigate the enemy's position to the east of Quingua in the vicinity of Bag Bag. Major Bell commanded the party, which consisted of a troop of the Fourth Cavalry, a Hotchkiss revolving cannon and one Hotchkiss mountain gun, in charge of John A. Anderson. They found a place where the river could be forded and discovered that the insurgents were strongly entrenched on the banks of the Bag Bag River. The country at this time was heavily timbered and the party was able to return unnoticed by the enemy.

A severe battle occurred on April 23rd as the forces closed in on Quingua. A reconnoitring party of cavalry encountered a large body of insurgents and the fire was so withering that Major Bell was forced to retire. Reinforcements of infantry were promptly called for and soon the Nebraskans moved forward to the fray. The fight lasted several hours, and the infantry and cavalry were forced to endure a heavy fire out in the open from a long line of Filipinos entrenchments hidden in a line of underbrush and trees. It was during this engagement that the gallant Stotsenberg was killed while rallying his men for the charge over the open. The artillery did not arrive until 11 o'clock, when two rifles, one from each battery under Captain Wedgewood and Lieutenant Critchlow came to the front and as usual soon ended the argument. Private D. J. Davis of Battery A was shot through the fleshy part of the leg, and while standing twenty yards behind the piece Captain Wedgewood was wounded in the hand and stomach by a flying piece of copper from the defective gun breech. The artillery occupied a position at one hundred yards range during this stubbornly fought engagement. The guns were partially sheltered by the foliage of a clump of trees to the left of the Pulilan road and the Nebraska infantry. Firing from the artillery was plainly effective, and after forty-five minutes of continual bombardment the insurgents retired over the Pulilan road toward Bag Bag.

During this engagement Lieutenant Fleming of the Sixth United States Artillery arrived from Malolos with one of his own and a Battery B gun, manned by a Utah detachment, and did valuable service at a one-thousand-yard range. As the natives retreated in columns they afforded a conspicuous target and bursting shrapnel tore large holes in the retiring lines. Private Abplanalp of Battery B, one of the drivers, was shot through the hand and arm while in the rear of the firing line.

This was considered to be as fierce a fight as that in which the rough riders won their way to glory at Las Guasimas. At that point three regiments were engaged and there were seventy casualties. At Quingua there were only five hundred Americans against a large body of insurgents and sixty of these were killed or wounded. General Gregoria del Pilar, the dashing young Filipino leader, who had previously visited General Otis for the purpose of arranging terms of peace, commanded the dusky warriors at this place. Though he was forced to retreat he took upon himself the credit of killing Colonel Stotsenberg, and afterwards boasted that he had slain one thousand Americans in the engagement.

The next morning Lieutenant Fleming with two big rifles and a Hotchkiss revolving cannon, in charge of Gunner Corporal M. C. Jensen, forded the Quingua River, a tributary of the Rio Chico, which in turn draws its waters from the Rio Grande de Pampanga, at Calumpit. The remainder of the artillery, consisting of a platoon of Battery A, under Lieutenant Naylor, and one gun under Lieutenant Critchlow, went on down the Pulilan road toward Bag Bag. There was a sharp encounter on this road, during which a body of the enemy about a thousand yards to the right attempted a flank movement, but a few shots from the big guns and the Hotchkiss forced them to change their course. The guns directly under Major Young on the other side of the river became involved about three hundred yards south of the enemy's long low line of earthworks at Bag Rag. Their entrenchments occupied the strip of land at the junction of the Rio Chico and the Bag Bag Rivers. When a reconnoitring party visited this place on April 7th the plain surrounding the Bag Bag was covered with bamboo and underbrush, but now all the plain was as clean and level as if it had been swept by a cyclone. Thus the entrenched Malays had cleared a spot which commanded the plains for miles around.

Infantry and artillery advanced from both sides of the Quingua—Hale with Fleming on the other side and Wheaton with Utah to the south. Soon the artillery was engaged on the Pulilan road, 225 yards from the enemy. At this time the infantry force was fifty yards in the rear, where it was masked from the enemy but could render no important assistance. The fire from the Tagalan entrenchments was murderous. While the artillery fire was as rapid as possible at least two responsive volleys came from the entrenchments after each shot. Private Max Madison fell, killed instantly, early in the action; Private Frederick Bumiller received a fatal wound through the hips. Two other cannoneers were hit in their attire by glance balls and all three of the big guns were cut with Mausers. In Lieutenant Critchlow's single detachment of eight men five were struck—two killed and one seriously wounded. Wheaton's line meanwhile bore in from the left and the artillery swung forward with the line until they were almost on the opposite bank from the enemy. The armoured train, equipped with Gatlings revolving cannon, pulled up at this point and turned loose its armament upon the enemy at a 200-yard range. The insurgents stubbornly fell back under the terrific fire.

On the opposite bank Corporal Jensen and his crew, sixty yards from the enemy's position, were ripping the low entrenchments with the revolving cannon. His position was perilous and his gallant fight soon ended. He was pierced through the stomach with a bullet and on the next day died from the wound. Lieutenant Fleming, in his report to the chief of artillery, says of him:

I desire especially to mention Corporal M. C. Jensen for gallantry in this action. His fearlessness undoubtedly cost him his life.

He also recommends in this report that Corporal Jensen be awarded a certificate of merit.

Calumpit is a city which the insurgents looked upon as invulnerable. Its huts and stone bridges are on both sides of the Rio Grande de Pampanga—the broadest and longest river in Luzon. It was here a few months before that the insurgents captured many thousand Spanish prisoners with all their arms, and they were prepared to vigorously contest the advance of the American troops.

The guns of Utah and the two big rifles of Lieutenant Fleming were on the south side of the Bag Bag, and it is only a mile from here to the Filipino stronghold. The advance began early on the morning of the 27th. A platoon under Lieutenant Naylor, who had been in charge of Battery A pieces since the wounding of Captain Wedgewood, one gun under Lieutenant Critchlow, Fleming's two guns and a Hotchkiss in charge of Corporal Bjarnson were pushed by hand over a bridge hastily constructed over the waters of the Bag Bag. The clattering din of the infantry could soon be heard in altercation with the insurgents at the front. The insurgents, behind entrenchments, were sending volleys fast into the Americans from the north bank of the Pampanga. It was observed that the long bridge had been partially destroyed and the rails torn from the track for several hundred yards. The heavy iron beams of the bridge were placed above the two lines of entrenchments. Iron rails supported the ponderous beams, and between them was formed a long slot for Filipino rifles.

The three big Utah guns were rushed to a position on the right of the station, about 100 yards from the enemy, and where there was partial protection from a *nipa* hut. Earthworks were quickly thrown up and to divert the enemy's attention while this was going on, a squad of Montana men kept up a constant fire from a position immediately in front of the artillery. Bullets came in sheets from the Filipino position. A Montana sharpshooter, shot through the head, fell dead at the foot of the half-made emplacement. Fleming's guns pointed through an aperture broken through the solid brick walls of the station facing the half-demolished bridge. Further off to the left Corporal Bjarnson with the revolving Hotchkiss was with the line of Kansas infantry under Colonel Funston. Out on the left Colonel Funston was performing the famed and intrepid feat by which he was able to cross the river. Protected by the swift fire of the revolving Hotchkiss, a Kansas man with a rope swam the swift moving waters of the Pampanga and fastened one end to the base of a bamboo tree. Then Funston with about forty of his men crossed the river on hastily constructed rafts, guided by the long ropes. Suddenly this small body of warriors charged and attacked the insurgents on the left flank. The insurgents who had valiantly and stubbornly held their position, were terrorized by the unexpected onslaught, and the whole line in the east side of the bridge sprang from the entrenchment and fled northward along the railroad embankment. Natives were strewn thick upon the banks of the river as they ran. A mounted Filipino officer was shot through the heart as he stood with flashing sword vainly trying to rally his confused and fleeing troops. The Tagalans to the right were touched with consternation and fled from their bulwarks. And so during this one hour Colonel Funston performed the most dashing deed of the war and the Malay hosts were driven from their strongest defence. Fifteen hundred American soldiers in this battle contested with 12,000 entrenched warriors of Luzon, and won by their prowess and the strategy of a gallant leader.

The two brigades were allowed to rest for several days on the sunny banks of the Pampanga. On May 14th the troops began the march toward San Fernando, which lies green and low at the base of Mt. Arayat, which can be seen for many miles around. The artillery, with the mules, crossed the river on rafts. Wheaton advanced up the railroad track while Hale's brigade strung out over the Apalit road.

A revolving Hotchkiss cannon and one Gatling gun, manned by Battery B detachments, were mounted on trucks. This moving battery was commanded by Lieutenant Naylor. As the troops approached Santo Tomas the insurgents were discovered, entrenched on both sides of the railroad. As the infantry engaged them on the right, Lieutenant Naylor's machine guns played on the thin line of smoke curling above the Filipino entrenchment. As the infantry pressed them on the right they retreated over the railroad towards a long line of entrenchments, and the bullets from the Gatling fell among them here faster than autumn leaves. Colonel Funston, at the head of his troops, took the fire line of entrenchments on the left of the track and moved down on the Tagalans, who had constructed a long line of entrenchments parallel with the railway. They were beaten back by the Kansas men, but in this charge Colonel Funston fell, having sustained a slight wound in the arm. During this engagement General Luna, most renowned of the Filipino chiefs, was wounded in the arm, and as there was only a light infantry fire, the opinion prevailed that this was inflicted by Lieutenant Naylor's fast-clicking Gatling gun. General Wheaton personally praised Lieutenant Naylor for his work in the Santo Tomas battle, and afterwards in his report recommended him for meritorious service.

Over on the right up the Apalit road Captain Wedgewood and Lieutenant Critchlow were encountering difficulties. The insurgents had constructed pitfalls in the road. They were thinly covered with a layer of leaves and earth and the wayward feet of mule and soldier were menaced beneath with sharp pointed wedges of bamboo. These were discovered early in the march and no accidents resulted from them. There was some brisk fighting on this end of the line and the big guns shelled the insurgents on the opposite side of the river. The whole of the next day was consumed in transporting the artillery and equipage across the river on a raft constructed by the engineers, and on May 6th they entered San Fernando.

This fair city was half destroyed by flames, and when the troops entered no lingering black warriors could be found. They had all retreated farther north, following in the general direction of the railway. Major-General MacArthur's headquarters were established near the centre of that part of the city which was untouched by the flames, and close by the Utah guns were parked. Later one of the big guns was utilized for outpost duty, a rather remarkable use for artillery. Every night after the Filipinos had begun to gather again near the city one of the pieces with a gun crew would go down a sunken road and watch all night with the farthest outposts of the infantry.

During this period Major-General Otis had issued an order offering thirty pesos to every Filipino warrior who would return his rifle to the American authorities. On May 23rd Major Bell went on an expedition up the railway track for the purpose of posting up the order, and took with him two troops of the Fourth Cavalry and a revolving Hotchkiss gun, manned by Sergeant Emil Johnson and Corporal Hesburg of Battery A and Private Martin of Battery B. All the men were mounted and the cannon equipped with a small Filipino horse, so that if necessary a hasty retreat could be made. They proceeded up the railway track, and notices were duly and conspicuously left at Bacalor and Quiuag. Just as the forces reached the outskirts of Santa Rita they were fired on by a large body of insurgents, who were heavily entrenched around the city. The revolving cannon was used effectively and Major Bell and his men went into action five times, but the insurgent attack was too fierce for the small force and it was obliged to retreat. With a whoop of joy the Filipinos rose from their trenches in pursuit, cheering loudly as they came. They followed for five miles through Bacalor, and as far back as their old entrenchments surrounding San Fernando. The rather meagre encouragement of having been able to chase a small troop of cavalry seemed to give the Tagalans at this time an idea that they had the whole American force in retreat.

During the night word was brought to General MacArthur that the Filipinos were preparing to make an attack early the next morning. At dawn the Montana and Kansas regiments and a platoon under Lieutenant Naylor went out to meet them. The Filipinos were in force in their old position to the northwest. The Kansas went through some cornfields on the left and the Montanas through a sunken road to the right. The artillery remained in a concealed position in the centre and waited until the two regiments had moved up on the startled natives from both flanks. As the insurgents retreated in confusion the big guns played on the scattered ranks. A large number of the natives were killed during this clever manoeuvre and thirty of their rifles were captured.

The Tagalans when on the warpath are persistent. The next day they occupied entrenchments farther to the north. They were again driven back and this time they took up a position towards Mexico and in front of the Iowa troops.

During the next few days the Malay hordes came toward San Fernando from all sides. Eventually their forces completely surrounded the city. General MacArthur watched their plans, saw them tearing up the earth for entrenchments and waited. It was apparent that they were preparing to march with crushing force upon the American troops.

The cloud burst on June 16th. Just at that time, when the

Americans were not looking for them, the Tagalans descended on the town. Captain Fred Wheeler was out on a plain drilling a troop of the Fourth United States Cavalry. It was in the morning and there was a heavy mist. One of Captain Wheeler's men informed him that he could see the niggers coming. The captain could see nothing and sent for his glasses, but before they arrived the long skirmish line of the Tagalans could be seen emerging like spectres from the mist. Then there was a remarkable spectacle—the Fourth Cavalry and the Tagalan warriors racing for the same entrenchments. The cavalrymen arrived first and there the battle began.

The natives came in from four sides. The outposts waited in the old Filipino entrenchments and on some parts of the line the attacked Tagalans were allowed to approach within 200 yards. Most of the guns, when the fight began were located close to MacArthur's headquarters, but they were soon on all parts of the line. When the attack by the Filipinos began the gun under command of Lieutenant Naylor was on its way to the outposts. It had been the custom to take the gun there just before dawn and bring it back immediately after darkness came. The advancing Filipinos began firing before the gun was in position. Corporal Hanson was in charge at the time, and the rifle was at once rushed to the emplacement. Word came at the same hour to Lieutenant Naylor, who was officer of the outpost, and he went through a heavy fire down the road leading to the entrenchment. When he arrived there the Filipinos were within three hundred and fifty yards and were advancing over the rice ridges at a rapid gait. The lieutenant had a shell sent into the approaching insurgents, who seemed astounded to find that the artillery occupied such an advanced position. When nine shells had been sent into their line, the Filipinos gradually drew back and were not seen any more on this part of the line during the fight.

The Seventeenth and Twenty-second Infantry were the support on this end of the line, which faced to the north.

On the west, east and part of the north line were the Kansas and Montana infantry. It was to this point that the two guns of Lieutenant Gibbs were moved when the firing began, and here the guns inflicted severe damage on the islanders. Another gun of Battery B

PREPARING FOR AN ENGAGEMENT

was also placed near this part of the line under Lieutenant Hines, but it was unnecessary from this position to use the artillery.

This fight was the first time the American soldiers during the whole campaign had repulsed an attack from behind entrenchments, and they laid back and smiled as the black men approached and then passed out some volleys that made the whole advancing line reel. When the Tagalans began to retreat under the awakened storm, the Americans followed, and as the Filipinos recoiled from one regiment they were broken against another. A company of the Twentieth Infantry located near Santo Tomas was almost cut off by the advancing column of the enemy, and a company of the Montana men was sent to its assistance. The fight lasted nearly two hours and the Filipino loss amounted to several hundred. The only casualty on the American side was a slight wound received by a Montana man, which shows clearly what the Americans could do in a contest with a black man under conditions more or less equal. Colonel Funston stated afterwards that a shell from one of Lieutenant Gibbs's guns had killed fifteen Filipinos.

The burying of dead Filipinos the next day was a tragic sight. Sixty-four were engulfed in one trench. They were brought up in caribou carts, and the American pulled them off with ropes and deposited them in the common grave.

There was another fight on the 22nd, but the Filipinos seemed to have lost their dash and courage of a few days before, and on this occasion the artillery was not called out.

A few days later word came that the Utah battalion was ordered home, and on the 24th day of June the Utah men boarded the train for Manila and were carried away from the smoke of war and the darkly fought battlefields of the East.

*   *   *   *   *

Sergeant John A. Anderson with one gun of Battery B and a rifle of the Sixth Artillery was in the flying column of General Lawton, who left a path of ashes around the Pampanga province and finally drove the insurgents from San Isidro with his detachment on the 21st of March and arrived on the same day at Bocaue. The order to march came on the 23rd and the sergeant was given a position on the left of the Thirteenth Minnesotas. From the brow of the hill above Norzagaray the guns began shelling at 1500 yards. The front line was silenced but at this point the natives made an effort to turn the right flank, and it was necessary to throw many shrapnel into the advancing insurgents column before it turned. The next day Norzagaray was entered after the place had been shelled, and during this slight advance the artillery was in action five times. Colonel Sommers personally commended the detachment on the accuracy of its gunnery and its promptness. On the 25th Ongaut was burned and on the 26th there was an engagement which lasted for some time below Baliuag. San Maguel was taken on the 4th, and on the 13th a few shells were thrown into San Isidro, but the insurgents, after repeated defeats, showed small resistance here and soon retreated.

On the 24th the artillery arrived with the infantry at Candaba, and the detachment remained quartered here until the order arrived for the Utah men to return to Manila. The plan of Lawton's campaign was for his troops to drive the insurgents towards Candaba, where they could be met by the advancing forces under Major Kobbe and the river gunboats. But when General Lawton came down to Candaba there were none but American soldiers there as the insurgents forces had disappeared in the interior.

Shortly after the arrival in Malolos the Utah men were joined by Corporal Dusenbury and two other men of Battery B. They with a revolving Hotchkiss cannon were picked up by General Wheaton early in his advance from Caloocan, and were highly praised by the general for the skill and efficiency they had shown in many dangerous places. General Wheaton showed his appreciation of the work of the guns by attaching several regular and Oregon infantrymen to the pieces, in order that they could be carried over rough places with the greatest possible dispatch.

CHAPTER 4

The Gunboats

No history of the Utah batteries will be complete without a narrative of the exploits of the gunboats. While the land forces performed their duties with great honour and are to be commended in every way possible, it must be remembered that a portion of the men were fighting on the water and did work of such a character that they won especial mention from those in charge when the big guns were hurling death and the Gatlings were barking fire at the opposing army.

At first the proposition of building gunboats was not at all popular with the authorities. Some opposed the scheme on the grounds that it could not be successfully accomplished with the limited means at hand and the rivers of Luzon to contend with. However, later developments attested that those who were the originators of the plan showed greater wisdom than their opponents.

Sometime prior to the breaking out of hostilities between the American forces and the natives General Otis conceived the idea of employing gunboats on the rivers and lakes for the purpose of opening up lines of communication between difficult portions of our own lines. The fact that the rivers were shallow was the one serious objection to the project, but this difficulty was eliminated by the adoption of light draught boats. The nature of the country in the vicinity of Manila and the other towns where the heaviest fighting took place is such that it was apparent to those who were aware of these conditions that this craft might be engaged in protecting the advance of the infantry and artillery; could hold the hostile bands in check until favourable positions could be taken, and be of wonderful service in the campaign.

The first vessel to engage in this kind of work was the *Laguna de Bay*, which has made a reputation never to be forgotten so long as the history of the war in the Philippines remains familiar to the American mind. This vessel is doubtless as well known as the *Olympia*, the flagship of gallant Admiral Dewey, and while there are those who fail to recall the fact that the *Boston* or the *Raleigh* took part in the attack on the Spanish in the bay of Manila, it is safe to assert that the operation of the *Laguna de Bay* and her sister craft will ever be fresh in the minds of those who have made even a casual study of the events which took place during the campaign carried on by the brave men from the youngest State in the Republic.

The *Laguna de Bay*, the first converted gunboat, was placed in commission on January, 1899. She was formerly used by the Spanish as an excursion boat on the body of water from which she derived her name and prior to the fall of Manila had been captured by the Filipinos and turned over to the United States. She was by no means a small craft considering her environments—shallow rivers and muddy bayous. She was 140 feet in length, 40-foot beam with a draught of four feet. When she was fitted out it was decided to give her some protection for the men, so her main deck, the upper deck, the pilot house and the Gatling battery, were protected by a double sheeting of steel. The many bullet marks on this light armour demonstrated afterwards the wisdom of this policy. At this point it may not be out of order to interpolate the fact that her companion gunboats were similarly protected, which accounts for the small list of casualties.

The armament of the gunboat consisted of two three-inch marine guns, two 1.65 Hotchkiss revolving cannon and four Gatlings. At first Lieutenant R. C. Naylor was in charge of the guns, while Captain Randolph of the Third United States Artillery commanded the vessel. In addition to the men from the Utah batteries, several were detailed from the various regiments to act as sailors, riflemen and cannoneers.

The boats which were added to the fleet were the *Oeste*, the *Napindan* and the *Cavadonga*. The last went into commission on May 6th and was commanded by Lieutenant William C. Webb. The crews of the vessel were made up of members of the Utah batteries and men from the Twenty-third United States Infantry, the First South Dakota Infantry and the Third United States Battery.

On the morning of February 5th the *Laguna de Bay* steamed up the Pasig to the town of Santa Ana while the Nebraska, California and Washington troops assaulted the enemy from the land. Twenty minutes after the boat turned her guns upon the town the principal buildings were in flames and the stricken garrison made all haste toward San Pedro Macati and Guadaloupe. Next she turned her attention to those portions of the enemy stationed in Bacoor and Mandaloya. Her forward guns tore great gaps in the enemy's earthworks and her Gatlings raked the trenches with so galling a fire that the foe was sent flying towards the woods in the region of Pasig with the Nebraska Infantry in speedy pursuit. The following morning the boat passed Santa Ana, where two three-inch Krupp guns had been captured by the Idaho troops, and reconnoitred the native position in the woods beyond. Late that afternoon she returned to Manila and replenished her coal bunkers, when she resumed her old position at the Nebraska landing.

March 7th the gunboat again passed Santa Ana and went up as far as Guadaloupe, where the First California was quartered. General Anderson came up the river in a launch and a consultation was held as to future operations. Nothing of moment happened that day, but on the morrow General King arrived on his way to Pasig for the purpose of demanding the surrender of the town. He desired the *Laguna de Bay* to await his return. A vigilant patrol was kept up that evening and during the night three shots were fired by sentries from the boat. The day following was uneventful, but on the 10th the *Oeste*, which was towing a *casco*, came alongside and stated that Colonel Stotsenberg had sent word that the insurgents were massing west of the camp of the Nebraska regiment.

It was on the 14th that word was received from Colonel DuBois of the Idaho regiment to hurry up stream at all speed. This was done and an effort made to anchor off the mouth of the Pateros, where the infantry fire was very brisk. Here it was that Lieutenant Harting met his death. Harting with four men got aboard and the line was dropped when the boat sank, being swept almost immediately under the gunwale of the *Laguna de Bay*. The three men forward grasped the gunwale and were saved, but the officer and the fourth man went down stream. Though the lieutenant was a good swimmer, no sign of him could be seen. He was heavily laden with revolver, belt and ammunition. Lieutenant Larson jumped overboard to rescue him, but was unable to get even a glimpse of him. His body was found two days later near General Otis's headquarters. The fourth man escaped by swimming ashore.

By order of the commanding general February 16th, Major Grant took command of the river force and Captain Randolph rejoined his regiment. The next day an assiduous fire was directed against San Pedro Macati with telling effect.

The commanders now decided that in case the forces stationed at Guadaloupe should be too strongly pressed by the enemy they should fall back to San Pedro Macati, setting fire to the convent and other principal buildings as they returned. In this instance the gunboat was to steam up above Guadaloupe. On Sunday, February 19th, this very thing was done though the insurgents as yet had made no advance. The soldiers left the convent after firing it. As the gunboat moved up the stream she met with a determined resistance. The opposing force repeatedly assailed her, but her Gatlings finally compelled them to withdraw. An unsuccessful effort was made to explode a quantity of nitro-glycerine in the convent by the use of percussion shell. The boat then advanced nearer the town where it engaged the insurgents on both sides of the river. Every gun now played upon the enemy's lines. In the course of twenty minutes twenty-five three-inch shells, 4200 Gatling, 1500 Krag-Jorgenson and 800 Springfields were expended. This spirited defence caused the prudent native to withdraw to a country less subject to leaden bullets, and the boat dropped down stream. In the afternoon Admiral Dewey visited the *Laguna de Bay* in quest of information, and while he was securing what he came after a Filipino sharpshooter began taking pot shots at the Admiral, who, being unprotected, decided he was far enough inside the enemy's lines and turned back.

At San Felipe Lieutenant Naylor was sent ashore on the following day to cut down some trees and burn some huts so the view of the boats' gunners would not be obstructed, which duty was performed under a straggling fire.

Admiral Dewey visited the gunboats on the 21st, stating he

would send two rapid-fire guns for the *Laguna de Bay*. That was the object of his visit, which was short. The same day General King and his staff came aboard and were taken up the stream. Word was soon afterward received that the Wyoming battalion was going to advance on the enemy near Guadaloupe on the left of the river early the following morning but as the gunboat was not in a position to aid in the expedition she remained inactive when the firing began the next morning.

On the day following Lieutenant Naylor again landed with a small force of men at San Felipe, where he set fire to the buildings and cut down trees which would have obstructed the view. Nothing occurred until the night of the 25th, when desultory firing was heard at San Felipe, and following this matters were unusually quiet until the night of March 1st. That day the insurgents were encountered at San Pedro Macati and the Gatlings, the three-inch and the 1.65-inch guns were brought into action. During the firing Sergeant Shea received a slight wound in the hand. A three-inch gun was disabled in this engagement. Two days later another conflict took place at the same point resulting in the complete defeat of the enemy, who was forced from his position after a severe bombardment.

The morning of March 4th opened cloudy with *Laguna de Bay* at San Pedro. A sharp skirmish soon began. The natives held their position for some time but were finally compelled to give way before the superior strength of the Americans. Under orders from General Wheaton the gunboat followed them and directed a deadly fire into the woods on both sides of the river. During the fight, which lasted several hours, the boat was frequently struck by the bullets of the enemy. It was during this encounter that Private John Toiza of the Third Artillery laid down his life. He was shot in the left breast, the bullet passing downward through his heart, killing him instantly. A shell also lodged in the 1.65-inch gun, disabling it for the time.

On March 5th Admiral Dewey again came alongside and stated that General Otis had declared he believed he would keep the gunboats down the stream if they did not cease fighting so much. Then the Admiral added with emphasis, "We ought to have three such boats."

Two days later when Hale's brigade made an advance upon the insurgents on the left, and the natives were hurried with great speed toward Mariquina and the San Mateo River, the *Laguna de Bay* again performed excellent service in flanking them and turning their left wing against our right.

Very early on the morning of March 13th the battle of Guadaloupe and Pasig opened, the attention of the guns on the boat being centred on Guadaloupe. Meanwhile Wheaton advanced his troops on the right to Patteros and along the Pasig. The advance to Guadaloupe began along the river with the gunboat in the vanguard. Two insurgents partially concealed in the bushes on the banks were taken prisoners and turned over to the Twenty-third Infantry. Sunken *cascos*, loaded with rock, were frequently encountered, but the boat avoided them with only a little delay. Generals Anderson and Wheaton moved up from the right and the gunboat started up the stream. Near the Mariquina River they met with a fierce fire from both sides of the stream but no one on the boat was injured. Two Filipino launches were noticed but they got away. A *casco* was found in which were the clothing of some Filipino officer and men. The wearers had escaped.

On the day following there was a brisk engagement at Pasig in which the town was bombarded with good effect, some thirty of the enemy being killed, while the remainder were sent flying in all directions.

Nothing of interest occurred until Wednesday, March 15th, when a *casco* manned by natives was chased down the river. She was overhauled but not until her crew had jumped overboard and swam ashore. The *Laguna de Bay* raised a white flag for the purpose of investigating, but the insurgents instead of recognizing it pivoted a sharp small rim fire upon the boat which answered with a heavy rain of shell and shrapnel.

Two days later an expedition, led by the gunboats, headed for Morong on the opposite side of the lake. Lieutenant Webb with a Gatling and twenty-four men went ashore to make a reconnaissance. This small detachment was followed by three infantrymen under Captain Pratt. Upon the advance of the Americans the enemy retreated quickly across the plain and disappeared in the shades of the mountains beyond. One thousand bushels of rice and three *cascos* were captured at this place and a letter from General Pilar directing a general advance on Pasig was also found. But few inhabitants remained in the town and upon questioning them it was learned that the Filipinos had several large launches on the Pagsanyan River.

Major Grant had long been working to interest General Lawton in favour of an expedition against Santa Cruz. Santa Cruz is situated on the eastern shores of the lake just behind the point of a mountain which juts out into the water. She is the agricultural centre of all the rich land on the eastern side of the island of Luzon. All the smaller towns of the surrounding country look up to her. She is the emporium to which all the farmers and travellers and merchants resort and from which they reap a bounteous harvest.

The insurgents had long since seized upon this important place as it furnished an inexhaustible supply of food for their armies. Besides being far out of the way and difficult of approach, she became the military station to which the famished and fatigued insurgents looked for support and rest. Major Grant early noticed the importance of the town and thereafter he laboured incessantly to bring about its capture by the Americans. Finally, on the 18th, he succeeded in getting a fleet of gunboats, launches and *cascos* headed that way. Captain Pratt and Lieutenant Franklin attempted to make a landing on the shore in front of the town, but they failed as the water was too shallow. Five miles farther up the beach they made a profitable landing at the mouth of the Pagsanyan River. However, as this was blocked with obstructions of bamboo and rock, no effort was made to sail up the stream until three days had elapsed. Then the impediment was removed.

During the time which intervened between the 21st and the 28th little was done with the exception of attending to some needed repairs on the boat. On the 28th the gunboat advanced to the south of the Balucan River, where another delay was caused by the obstructions placed there by the natives. The country skirting this place was thickly covered with brush and low trees, very much like bayou. When about a mile and a half up the stream the enemy opened fire at a range of about 500 yards, which was returned by the guns on the boat. The fire was heavy and the insurgents evidently concluded that they were too close for comfort, for their fire slackened materially in a very short time. The *Laguna de Bay* and the *Napindan* then came down the stream. As the latter started to follow the larger boat the pilot was hit in the hand by a bullet and before he could recover himself the little craft had run aground. When the *Laguna de Bay* went to her assistance she also struck a bar and was held fast. The boats were compelled to remain here under fire until the tide came in and floated them off.

The work of the gunboats was without extraordinary interest until April 8th. On that day the fleet steamed up Pasig with twenty *cascos* and seven launches in tow. One thousand five hundred men, with two days' rations, two light artillery guns and necessary horses, composed the expedition, which was commanded by General Lawton. Among the troops were detachments from the Fourth United States Cavalry, the Fourteenth United States Infantry, the North Dakota, Idaho and Washington volunteers, the Sixth Artillery and the Signal Corps. This force reached Jalajala on the 9th and then awaited the arrival of the entire fleet. The place of advancement and attack—Santa Cruz—was mapped out and then the fleet steamed ahead. About five miles from Santa Cruz the *Napindan* ran into a point close to the shore and opened fire. Here the works were silenced, after which the troops landed. Under cover of the guns of the *Oeste* other men also disembarked. With Lawton aboard, the *Laguna de Bay* advanced toward the town approaching to within 300 yards of the shore. Some troops in *cascos* were put ashore. After a survey of the situation the boats went out into deep water and advanced from the right, while the troops encamped to the west of the town.

The next day a general advance began at daylight. The American forces came up to the enemy's position and opened fire. This was a signal for action on the part of the boats and after moving in closer they opened a heavy fire on the insurgent works. The troops placed south and west under General Lawton drove the natives northward while those posted along the shore of the river, aided by the guns on the boats, did considerable damage. Large bodies of the natives broke for a place of safety and while attempting to escape through a marshy open field many of them were killed. Shells actually mowed them down in heaps. By this time the lines of the infantry had been completely formed for an advance and the gunboats ceased their work. Shortly afterward our forces took possession of the town, and a message was received from Lawton saying he had established his headquarters in the church.

On the 11th the boats steamed up the lake and ran close to the shore near the mouth of the Pagsanyan River, where they opened fire on the town of Lumbaog, toward which the land forces were advancing. This fire was kept up until the infantry reached the place and took it. A message was received from General Lawton to the effect that he had captured the town of Pagsanyan; also that six launches had been captured there and were at the town. The *Cavadonga* at this time sailed up and relieved the *Oeste*. The guns were on the hills north of Orani and after a time the infantry took possession, for a flag from the church tower called for a boat to be sent to that place. The *Laguna de Bay* responded, went up the river and shelled Paite and Sinilaon until darkness ended her usefulness for that day. The troops had in the meantime checked the native advance and camped at Paite.

From this time until May 7th little was done by the boats. A greater part of the time was spent in making necessary repairs. On the last mentioned date a Macabebe named Soteros Gatdula reported for duty as pilot, and under his direction the fleet steamed across the bay to the mouth of the Rio Grande. Passing up this stream the boats shelled the towns of Guagua and Sexmoan. At the former place a fire had been started and a launch in the river was observed to be in flames. A party was sent out to try to save this craft, but she proved to be of little value and the attempt was abandoned. Two Spaniards claiming to have been held as prisoners by the natives, and a Filipino suspect were taken aboard.

It was decided early in May to make an effort to pierce the waters of the Rio Grande de Pampanga, which leads to Calumpit and beyond far into the heart of the enemy's country. The first efforts to search out the channel were made by the *Cavadonga* on May 9th. Soteros Gatdula, a Macabebe pilot, was directed by General Otis to undertake the task and the *Cavadonga* started on the cruise into the unknown waters early in the morning. Near the mouth of the river the boat suddenly went aground, and when the tide rose, and early in the day the boat was joined by the *Laguna de Bay*. The channel was then located by the Macabebe and there was no further difficulty in forcing a passage up the wide waters of the river, the largest on Luzon Island. For a long distance up the river the territory is occupied by the Macabebes, the ancient and traditional enemies of the Tagalan race. A large crowd of these friendly natives was on the shores of the river as the boats passed up and they filled the air with cheers and cries of *"Viva los Americanos,"* which the soldiers replied to in variegated and wonderfully woven Filipino phrases. One obstruction was met in the river consisting of cocoanut poles, but the Macabebes assisted in removing these from the path of the boats. Without having fired a shot, early in the afternoon the boats arrived at Calumpit, where troops of the infantry were stationed.

On May 14th the *Cavadonga* was sent out on a reconnoitring expedition up the river. On the way up Sexmoan and Apilit were passed, and it was observed that all the natives fled from the river as soon as the gunboat approached. The country is heavily timbered on both sides of the river, and there was no evidence of a hostile attitude on the part of the natives until the boat swung round the curve leading to San Luiz. Almost through the entire distance the shores were lined with Filipino entrenchments, but it was discovered that these were unoccupied. Lieutenant Webb was out on the bow capstan, entirely unsheltered by the meagre 3-16-inch armour with which the craft was encased. Just as a curve was rounded in front of San Luiz a long line of straw hats and the bores of fifty rifles were seen facing the boat from the port side, no more than fifty yards away. Lieutenant Webb was scanning the opposite shore with his glasses, when the lookout discovered the enemy on the port side. Sergeant Ford Fisher called out a sudden warning to the lieutenant and reached out towards him. Just then the volley came. Fisher reeled backward with a bullet piercing his brain. Instantly the bow one-pounder and the Gatling gun on the port side tore the Filipino entrenchments. Bullets pelted fast against the slight armour of the cruiser. Fred Mitchell, one of the men at the Gatling gun, was wounded in the hand. The *Cavadonga* turned round almost where it stood and slowly moved back, and during a wonderful skirmish in which the native and American frequently fired in each other's faces at a range of twenty yards, raked the Filipino works with the fast-firing machine guns. The fighting only lasted thirty minutes.

When it was over Ford Fisher, who was still breathing, was placed on board the *Oceania*, which had remained about two hundred yards in the rear during the fighting, and almost at the moment he was laid on the craft he expired. The *Oceania* sped quickly down the river with the dead body of the sergeant, but frequently the *Cavadonga* stopped to suppress the desultory fire from the natives who had fled during the early part of the action. It was learned afterwards from the "padre" at San Luiz that fifty insurgents had been killed during the engagement, and when the Utah men arrived there a few days later a long line of new graves in the walled cemetery told a tragic story of the ending of the fight. On the evening of this day the Seventeenth Regular Infantry and a battalion of the Ninth Infantry advanced up the Rio Grande from Calumpit over the old Apilit road under the leadership of Major Kobbe of the Third United States Artillery. Early the next morning the *Laguna de Bay* and *Cavadonga* started up the river and most of the way kept within view of the troops on the shore. Occasionally the gunboats moved ahead and daring scouts could be seen calmly looking into vacated Filipino entrenchments. The enemy was encountered several times along the shore as far as San Luiz and all entrenchments were bombarded by the *Laguna de Bay* some distance to prevent a repetition of the disastrous surprise of the day before. When San Luiz was neared white flags could be seen floating everywhere, and on arriving there it was discovered that the whole body of insurgents had disappeared into the interior. The boats remained at this position during the night, and early the next morning resumed the advance ahead of the infantry up the waters of the Pampanga. During this journey large numbers of Filipinos were met in *cascos* with their families and all their earthly possessions, making their way down the stream. About noon the boats reached Candaba without a hostile shot having been fired during the whole day. Here Major Grant was met by the Mayor of the city, who stated that he had forced the soldiers to evacuate in order to prevent the bombardment of the town and the subsequent loss of life among the people of whom he was guardian. An evidence of the hasty departure of the natives was found upon entering the town, for a guard list giving the names of the officers and enlisted men of the guard was found posted on the walls of the town hall.

This ended the fighting record of the gunboats under a Utah commander. From this period until June 24th the boats were utilized in carrying supplies and towing soldiers, laden *cascos* and wounded men up and down the Pampanga. On May 24th the rebel commissioners, General Gregoria del Pilar and Colonel Actia, who had gone to Manila to negotiate peace with General Otis after the crushing defeat of the insurgents at Calumpit, were taken on the gunboats and conveyed as far as Candaba. They had expressed a wish to go by way of the gunboats, as they had no desire to cross the insurgents' lines at San Fernando because General Luna was in command at that place and there was strife between the two generals. Pilar showed great interest in the armament of the *Laguna* and said he would give all his wealth for one of the three-inch guns. The *Oceania* was sent ahead with instructions to all the commanding officers to make as large a display as possible. At San Luiz the instructions were not complied with and as the *Laguna* passed one officer and four men were falling in for guard. General Gregoria smiled. Farther up the river the case was different. Where they were in the habit of posting but one guard there was an officer and twenty men. This was repeated at all the other stations until Candaba was reached. General Gregoria's smile had faded, and he remarked that the Americans kept the country better patrolled than he had imagined. The general and colonel were landed at Candaba and under an escort of Americans disappeared in the distant green line of woods.

On May 24th it was known among all the Utah men that their days of fighting were over, and on this date Major Grant was relieved of his command of the river boat fleet. And so ended, for Utah, the career of these wonderful ironclad river machines.

CHAPTER 5

The Homecoming

While the fighting Utah batterymen were still living in the *nipa* huts at San Fernando and Baliaug and repelling the attacks of the dusky Tagalan braves at Candaba and Morong from General Otis an order came to the Cuartel. It had an unpretentious look—that slip of paper; but it carried a message of great importance to the belligerent Utahn than any he had received since the thunders of war shook the earth on the night of February 4th. It told the artilleryman to gather all his portable utensils and board the United States transport *Hancock*, which lay idly in the bay waiting orders to weigh anchor and steam for America.

Almost a week passed before the scattered batteries were assembled within the familiar walls of the Cuartel. The main body at San Fernando turned over its guns to the famous Third Artillery and arrived safely at the quarters over the Manila and Dagupan railroad; Lieutenant Seaman's detachment at Baliaug dropped its war machinery and made all possible speed to Manila; Lieutenant Webb's detail on the *Cavadonga* for the first time turned its back on the enemy and fled for the protecting walls of the barracks. When these battle-begrimed veterans reached the quarters there was such a demonstration as the old walls had never seen before. The old scenes of order disappeared, the rigors of discipline were relaxed, and chaos reigned. Everything was made subservient to the one all-absorbing topic, *home*. The sturdy soldier doffed his war attire and donned his peaceful garb. The renowned Utah band paraded the streets in holiday dress and, with the blare of brass, proclaimed the happy news to the nut-brown maid. The stalwart warriors danced and sang to the music of that soul-lifting song, *A Hot Time in the Old Town Tonight*. The jubilant battle hero collected his ordnance and other war trappings and handed them over to the ordnance officer while he exchanged looks of mutual doubt and suspicion with that important personage. The weary and worn Utahn bade adieu to the dreamy-eyed damsel of the East with many expressions of fond attachment and love; then mustered his heterogeneous troop of relics and curiosities and joined the Nebraska regiment on the *Hancock*. Two days later the officers steamed over from the gay apartments of the *Baltimore* in a brightly decorated launch and walked aboard the big boat. Finally a goodly supply of canned beef and antiquated swine were hoisted on the vessel and the captain gave orders for the sailing flag to be put to the breeze. This was on July 1st.

When the official contingent was safely housed in spacious staterooms it was learned that quite a change had taken place in the roster of that worthy body. The shoulders of Captain Grant were adorned with the gold leaf of a major; Lieutenant Critchlow had been elevated to a captaincy; Lieutenant Naylor wore the single bar of a first lieutenant, and First Sergeant John A. Anderson of Battery B shone in the glowing uniform of a second lieutenant. Major Young sent a letter bidding farewell to the Utahns and expressing his disappointment at not being able to accompany the batteries home.

The batteryman entertained no high opinion of the Government transport. He had become acquainted with the luxuries which Uncle Sam provides the defenders of his broad acres. He had already learned how elaborately the American Government furnishes apartments for its soldiers and food for its larder. So, after he had landed safely on the main deck and deposited his knapsack and monkeys, he was not surprised when the order came for him to take his goods and chattels and repair to the forward hold. He entered the gangway and descended four flights of stairs without any misgiving or hesitation. He threaded his way through the labyrinthine passage of his subaqueous home with a skill equal to that displayed by the blind fish of the Mammoth Cave. He beheld the wonderfully constructed bunks which glowed spectre-like in the semi-darkness without evincing the least disappointment. Later when one of these had been assigned as his sole property during the voyage he accepted it and its diminutive proportions without a murmur and philosophically concluded that the Government either thought he had diminished in stature while on the islands or intended to reduce his dimensions on the way home. Thus the Utah warrior was quartered. The celerity with which he adapted himself to his environments clearly exhibited his excellent training. He quickly disposed of the problem of how to shorten his linear measurements to four feet eight inches by placing himself diagonally across his bed. The posture thus assumed was not unlike that of a skeleton in armour. When his joints became cramped he straightened himself out by throwing his soles against the head of his neighbour, who instantly developed a remarkable vocabulary of explosives anent Hades, Paradise, Satan, etc.

Mess time on the *Hancock* was not an occasion of the greatest felicity to the returning volunteers. Their epicurean tastes could not totally harmonize with bogus coffee and cows that had a flavour strangely akin to that of horse flesh. When the bugle shrilly proclaimed the dinner hour the men formed in a long serpentine line and displayed their skill in keeping their equilibrium and at the same time holding their place in the procession. The rattle of Government tinware, upon which the soldier had inscribed many strange hieroglyphics descriptive of his adventures, served as a musical entertainment in lieu of the melody furnished at all other times by the combined efforts of the Utah and Nebraska bands. They facetiously derided the commissary sergeant who had long since become calloused to all sneering remarks made by the ordinary defender of the flag; for in case of any exceedingly hostile demonstration he was armed with a long cleaver and several carefully concealed bolos. They made comments, too, not at all flattering to the bill of fare, about "gold fish" and "slumgullion" and ancient swine, but they "wasted their venom on a file." The cooks, also, came in for a share of the complimentary criticisms, for they were not blessed with a superabundance of skill in the culinary art. Occasionally the voice of a volunteer was raised in loud-mouthed protest over the meagreness of his own supply of food and the apparent excessiveness which adorned the plate of his associate. This always ended in a peculiar panegyric on the merits of a person who had a "stand in" or a "pull" with the officers. When the ravenous Utahn was handed his cheer the bestower very kindly warned him not to taste or smell the victuals, as such an act would be attendant with serious injury to his appetite; so he merely devoured the contents of his plate with his eyes and passed them on to his gastronomical organs with no further ceremony.

A small portion of the forward deck was allotted to the batteries to be used as a mess hall, lounging apartment, etc. It was here the battle-scarred veterans collected at meal times and dispatched their slender store. As the Pacific is not always so peaceful as its name, this pleasing task was not at all times accomplished with ease. When on a boat tipped to an angle of 60 degrees, a Japanese juggler would find some difficulty in conjuring his body to remain in an upright position and simultaneously inducing a seething plate of soup to abide in a placid state; yet the uninitiated volunteers contrived to perform this daring feat three times a day. The many strange figures which they described in their endeavours to execute these occult tricks would have done justice to the most skilful acrobat. Frequently, as the vessel gave an extra lurch, the insecure warrior proceeded with all possible speed to the side of the boat and deposited his food and eating utensils on the surface of the sad sea waves amid the execrations of those whom he had the good fortune to come in contact with on his hasty trip and the jibes of his appreciative audience. At this same place the mendacious batterymen gathered in the warm afternoons to tell sea serpent legends and fairy stories about some great event which had never happened in the trenches. When this supply had been exhausted they began forthwith to dilate upon the virtues of the most famous officers until those worthies would have been unable to recognize their own characters had they been confronted with them in their garnished garb. Once in a very great while an officer strolled down from the aristocratic atmosphere of the saloon dining hall and watched the feeding of the enlisted with a superior grace. To convince the famished soldiers that they were getting a redundant quantity of food, he sometimes called for more than was needed to be cooked and then there was always a good heap of hash left to show the astonished men that they were merely chronic kickers. Then the well-fed comedian adjourned to his spacious saloon and offered an apology to his offended stomach by supplying it with an abundance of all that the steamer carried.

The one great comfort to the fagging spirits of the Utahn was the battery fund. Through the darkest days of war his dying hopes were revived by visions of what the future held in store for him by the aid of this phantom. It was to the despairing volunteer what mirage is to the thirsty traveller of the desert. The fund represented the combined contributions of the soldiers, benevolent persons and charitable institutions. Besides this a fabulous sum was added by the artillery canteen which exchanged beer for the Utes' money and, in addition to what it contributed towards the battery fund, provided turkeys and succotash for the Thanksgiving and Christmas banquets. When it was announced that this enormous sum was to be expended for dainties on the way home the joy of the batteryman knew no limits. Spectre dinners of mutton, cakes and pies arose in his mind with a suddenness that would have startled the most ardent disbeliever in ghosts. Without the aid of Pluto he called up all the spirits of meals long dead and fed on them till the marvellous distribution should take place. And it was not long in coming. One morning, accompanied by the stentorian voice of the bugle Judge Williams, heavily laden with a huge cargo of jam, hove in sight. Then were many whispered comments made about the quantity which each man was to receive. The Judge soon stopped this and shortly after there was a hum of satisfaction all along the deck as the men made way with this delicacy. Now the gastronomy of the warrior lived and flourished under the rigors of army hardtack and navy beans, but it collapsed at once when introduced to Jamesson's jam. There was a sudden epidemic of cramps throughout the entire organization, but the ever victorious commissary sergeant soon stamped this out by the judicious application of some French mustard, which had been purchased by the battery fund. And thus the men of Utah were fed.

Meanwhile the swift *Hancock* steamed out of Manila bay and speeded toward Japan. Two days out she passed the beautiful Island of Formosa, and in three days more the vessel came in sight of Nagasaki, the leading coaling station of the Flowery Kingdom. Just at dusk the pilot boarded the vessel and directed her safely through the narrow channel into the land-locked harbour. Next morning all the soldiers were given shore leave for the day and *san-pans*—the native craft—were provided to take the men ashore. Here the Utahn explored the country in the *jin-rickisha*—a two-wheeled vehicle which is drawn by the cabby himself, who as soon as he has settled to his satisfaction the price to be paid, ambles off at a gentle speed. If the Island of Kiusiu appeared beautiful as the boat approached it in the waning twilight it seemed doubly so in the glory of the morning sun. It is a land where poetry breathes as freely as the gentle zephyrs blow from the summit of Mount Olympus; it is a land where women are as fair as the daughters of Niobe. The pretty terraced hills adorned with Pagan temples are rich in the odour of the spice and pine; the pellucid lakes and bays gather a silver purity from the very crest of the mountain; and as one gazes upon this beauty and simple grandeur he imagines that it was just such influences as these that stirred the soul of Hellas when she pictured Aphrodite springing out of the sea or Neptune riding in his chariot of shells with a gay company of Tritons and Nymphs. Three days, owing to a raging typhoon, the vessel was delayed in coaling, but after the storm had spent its force the coaling was resumed and the transport put to sea. On the 11th the ships arrived at Muji, the key to the southern end of the inland sea. Here Japan's military power is fully shown. Huge guns bristle from every hill, dark warships stud the clear waters of the ocean and soldiers deck the peaks. The sharp green cliffs in the inland sea chop off into the water and from every one of these of any importance a cannon menacingly points. Both entrances to the place are controlled by powerful fortresses which command the open sea for a distance of twelve miles. In such a way has the Mikado prepared for any war emergency. Two days after sighting Muji the *Hancock* dropped anchor in the harbour of Yokohama. The visit here lasted three days, during which the Utahns took a trip to Tokyo and saw of what the outside wall of the Emperor's palace is composed. At Yokohama the batterymen spent the time in visiting the European portion of the town and learning all they could about the flavour of the Japanese foods.

On the 16th the vessel lifted her ponderous anchor and pointed her prow eastward.

The only exciting incident during the entire voyage happened at Nagasaki, when the first officer attempted to use corporal punishment on the ship's quartermaster who had been ashore and in addition to getting drunk had succeeded in breaking his kneepan. While he was getting his wound attended to in the ship's hospital the big burly mate descended the gangway and struck him a violent blow in the face. Not content with this brutal treatment the monster had the poor wretch placed in irons and dragged up the ship's ladder. Just as this procession landed on the upper deck the soldiers rose unto a man and stopped the performance amid cries of "throw him overboard." Surprised and astounded at this interference the worthy officer demanded of the mob if they knew they were mutinying. To which several of the leaders answered they knew not under what legal nomenclature such a demonstration could be classed but that they would carry out their threat to the letter if the castigation should proceed. At this the cowed dignitary retreated in haste to the security of his cabin.

The *Hancock* was generally regarded as a fast boat. This may have been true twenty years before the Nebraskans and Utahns boarded her, but there were those who doubted the truth of such an assertion. During her infancy on the Atlantic the boat had struck an iceberg and succeeded in breaking forty feet off her bow. Since then she has been subject to periodical disturbances in her interior, consequently her owners patiently awaited the advent of war, knowing that the United States Government would purchase her for the transport service at an early opportunity. It is needless to say she eventually found her way into the Pacific. On leaving Manila it was the intention of the *Hancock* to break her own record of eighteen days between San Francisco and that port. Her new record of thirty days had not yet been announced in the newspapers. As a matter of fact she did happen to break her machinery and delay the expedition six hours, causing a break in the fond hopes which the soldiers had built up.

There was one death during the trip over, Richard Ralph of Battery B, who died at Nagasaki of typhoid fever on the 15th of July. Corporal George Williams of the same organization was also left at the same point owing to a severe attack of the dysentery. Both men were Englishmen and had enlisted at Eureka. Otherwise the health of the batteries was good.

The big prow of the *Hancock* loomed up darkly on the night of the 29th in San Francisco harbour and rested at anchor. The long sea journey was over. Until very late that night, long after taps had sounded sharply over the waters of the harbour, the soldiers clustered around the deck of the ship, heard the megaphone dialogues between the newspaper tugs and the transport, and looked with longing eyes and hearts that beat with joy at the gleaming lights of San Francisco.

Many friends from Utah arrived on tugs during the next day, when the transport was still in quarantine, and there was a generous greeting when the transport moved up to the dock on the morning of the 30th. The whole of this day was spent by the soldiers in exchanging greeting with friends and in preparing their property for transportation to the Presidio.

It was on the morning of the 31st that the soldiers were permitted for the first time to descend from the transport and walk again, after sixteen months of absence in the Orient, upon the shores of the United States.

The battalions marched up the streets of San Francisco behind the veterans of the Nebraska regiment, the centre of a tremendous demonstration. At the Presidio they were given quarters on the slopes to the left of the Presidio road. The patriotic sentiments and generous feelings of the citizens had been further shown, as the slopes of the hills were lined with large Sibley tents, each equipped with a stove as protection from the chilly mists that creep up by night from the bay. There were also frame buildings for use as offices and a large kitchen and mess room, commodiously and thoroughly equipped for comfort and convenience.

The citizens of Utah in the meantime had been active in preparations for receiving the native warriors. On August 8th, Adjutant-General Charles S. Burton and Colonel Bruback, members of the governor's staff, and representing the citizens' committee, arrived at the Presidio and used every effort in providing for the further comfort of the men and arranging for their early departure to their homes in Utah. It was learned that a special train had been chartered by the citizens to convey the volunteers to Utah, and to the fund necessary for this purpose Collis P. Huntington of the Southern Pacific had contributed $2500.

The date for the muster out of the Utah troops was fixed by the headquarters of the Department of California as August 16th, and notwithstanding the efforts of General Burton and Major Grant to have this time extended, General Shafter was unable to give an extension of time. This left but a short period for the immense labour of closing the affairs of the battery and the intricate details of the muster out. The captains of the batteries and a large clerical force were kept working almost continuously from the day of the arrival at the Presidio, and late on the night of the 15th they had the gratification, after toilsome days and sleepless nights, of putting the final touch to the muster out rolls. The next morning the rolls went to the paymaster. The labours of the Utah volunteers in the army of the Republic were over.

Some time before this, on August 5th, the men passed the final physical examination, and the general condition of the command was found to be extraordinarily good. Then the men were ready for the last function of muster out.

The next day the paymaster's wagon rattled up the Presidio slope. Then the soldiers performed the last act of their soldier career. One by one they marched into the small official frame building where the paymaster fingered his gold. As the veterans came out, each hand laden with gold, there was upon each face an iridescent smile, not only because of the augmented wealth, but for the reason that each one knew that for him the last bugle call had sounded, that his breast would no longer swell under the blue of the United States uniform. In two hours the soldiers had all left the Presidio, officers were shaking hands with the men over the bridged chasm of official dignity, and up on the slope of the Presidio the Sibley tents were ransacked and deserted.

That night the men of Utah slept in the hotels of San Francisco and dreamed of the morrow.

On the night of the 16th the transport *Warren* arrived, bearing among its passengers Major Richard W. Young, late chieftain of the batteries, who had come, much to the satisfaction of the men, in time to join his old war comrades in the homegoing.

The ferry which was to carry the soldiers to Oakland was ready before noon on the 17th, and early in the afternoon the engine of the special train gave a few premonitory puffs and the train full of returning warriors was moving towards Utah. The cars consisted of tourist sleepers for the men and a buffet Pullman for the officers and their friends. Across the centre car a streamer stretched, bearing the words, "The Utah Batteries."

Crowds gather at all the stations on the route and cheer the warriors. There was some delay, but nothing of special import occurred during the trip.

Early on the 19th the soldiers were able to see for the first time the towering blue mountains of Utah and the splendour of her sunshine. It was nearly noon when the train drew up at the Ogden station, and the soldiers looked out over the heads of a cheering multitude and listened to shrill whistles signalling a joyous welcome. The reception here only lasted an hour, but was cordial in the extreme, and out on the Ogden park a tempting lunch was served by fair women of Ogden. Lieutenant George A. Seaman, formerly of Ogden, was given an ovation as he stepped down from the platform of the car. A special car conveying the governor and a large party met the volunteers.

Two hours later the jubilation was complete. The volunteers saw at first a crowd and then a throng. They saw flaming streamers, flags fluttering and hats waving; they heard the diaphanous shriek of the steam whistles, the blaring of bands and the din of thousands cheering—all mingled in one chorus of praise and rejoicing. There were hurried handshakes and greetings and policemen's voices raised in fierce altercation with the crowd.

Soon with the cavalrymen and the engineers and the national guardsmen the batterymen had struggled into line. Horses were in waiting at the station for the officers and all were mounted in the parade. When the order to march could be heard through the tumult, the procession moved through a gaily decked arch at the station, and Majors Young and Grant rode side by side at the head of the battalion.

The crowd became more dense as the march continued towards Main street, and as far as Liberty Park thousands thronged the avenues. Excited relatives made a military formation impossible by rushing into the ranks to grasp the hand of a veteran.

At the Park the day's ceremonies were held. There were speeches by the governor and the two majors, and here the silver medals which the Legislature decided should be presented to the fighting sons of the State were awarded. With the conclusion of the formal exercises, the volunteers were led to an elaborately prepared lunch on beflowered tables beneath the shadows of the locust trees, and while refreshments were being taken fair maidens who ministered at the feast pinned badges on the breasts of the modest volunteers.

That night the celebration reached its full blazonry. The city glowed and sparkled; gaily-bedecked, her flaunting colours were aurioled in the lustres of the night; like an imperial palace, awaiting the return of victorious princes, the lights gleamed and burned into the darkness; and in the centre a luminous monument, glowing like the smile of an archangel, stood in vivid brightness the arch of triumph.

When the men of Utah batteries passed out into the darkness that night from the dazzle of colour they knew that the glamour of the victorious home-coming, the shouts and the jubilation were over. Yet there was peace in their hearts and on their breast was a badge of honour from a grateful people. And when they slept that night there were in their dreams no spectral visions of distant battlefields. All that was closed.

Officers of the Batteries

MAJOR RICHARD W. YOUNG

Major Richard W. Young, who left Utah as the ranking officer of the two batteries, being at that time captain of Battery A, and who was afterward appointed major commanding the battalion and still later selected as Associate Justice of the Supreme Court of Manila, is a native of this State, having been born April 19, 1858, his parents being Joseph A. Young (deceased), a son of the late Brigham Young, President of the Mormon Church, and Margaret Whitehead Young, who survived her husband.

Major Young is a trained military man, having been educated at the military academy at West Point. For a time after his graduation he was a member of the staff of Major-General Hancock, at that time commanding the Department of the East. Later he acted as Judge-Advocate in the army and conducted the Swaim court-martial, which was a case celebrated at that time. He was then transferred to the Third Artillery and stationed here with his battery at Fort Douglas. He resigned the service to take up the practice of law, which he engaged in until he was selected as manager of the Herald, a place which he filled acceptably for some time, when he again resigned to practice law.

At the outbreak of the war with Spain he tendered his services to the Government and was later selected by the governor of Utah to command Battery A. At Camp Kent he was the ranking officer and had entire charge of its affairs.

His services in the Philippines were of such a distinguished character that he was breveted major by the President and later promoted to the complete rank.

When the batteries' term of service was nearly completed, he was designated by Major-General Otis as Associate Justice of the Supreme Court of Manila and came home with the volunteers to enjoy a vacation.

Major Young is the author of a standard work on military law written while he was a lieutenant in the regular army. He is an able young man and one well liked and respected. He is exceedingly popular here in this city and State and outside of it.

His married life has been very happy. Eight children have been born to him and Mrs. Young, seven of whom are living.

MAJOR FRANK A. GRANT

Frank A. Grant, who went away from Salt Lake City with the bars of a captain, came home with the gold leaves of a major in his shoulder strap. He is not a native of this State, but was born in Kingston, Ontario, forty-four years ago. He received his education at the military college of his native city and graduated therefrom. After leaving school he came to the United States, where he became a citizen, and settling at Detroit was engaged by one of the large steamship companies in the capacity of pilot. He was a well trained man in his business and followed the occupation for a period of ten years. He has lived in Utah for ten years. During that time he was engaged in real estate and insurance business, in both of which he made great successes.

At the time of the breaking out of hostilities he was a member of the National Guard of Utah, being colonel of the First Infantry. Previous to this time he had held a position as staff officer on the brigade commander's staff, and was always a valuable man in military matters. It was due principally to his efforts that Troop C was organized in this city and made a success.

Governor Wells commissioned him as captain of Battery B, and with that rank he went into the field. Like Major Young he was breveted by the President for distinguished service and later was promoted to the full rank of major, coming home in command of the battalion.

As commander of the river fleet Major Grant performed excellent service, his expedition up the Rio Grande de Pampanga being especially well carried out. Since his return he has gone into his old business—that of insurance—and expresses himself as having had enough of military life. He is married and has six children.

Captain E. A. Wedgewood

Captain E. A. Wedgewood, who was promoted to the command of Battery A after the promotion of Major Young, left the State as First Lieutenant of Battery B. He is a native of Massachusetts, about forty years of age and an attorney-at-law, being the junior partner of the firm of Rawlins, Thurman, Hurd & Wedgewood. Immediately prior to his coming to Utah he had served as Sheriff for several terms in the State of Nebraska. He selected Provo for his home on coming to Utah and after entering the law office of George Sutherland in that city and being admitted to the bar, associated himself with Hon. S.R. Thurman. Later on the present firm was formed.

Captain Wedgewood was the officer sent back from San Francisco to Utah to recruit 104 men in order to bring the batteries to their full strength. Upon returning to San Francisco the party embarked and joined the commands in Manila.

Captain Wedgewood was a member of the National Guard prior to the time of his enlistment, being captain of the Provo company at the State encampment the year previous. He is said to be a most versatile character and can do anything from playing the violin to patching a sail or pleading a case in court. It was expected he would rejoin the National Guard, but it is learned he has had enough of military honours and will engage in the practice of his profession with a view to reaping *shekels* for use in his old age.

CAPTAIN JOHN F. CRITCHLOW

Captain John F. Critchlow left the State with the batteries a second lieutenant. He came back here leading Battery B. His promotion was due to distinguished service performed while abroad. He was specially recommended for gallantry by Major Young and for coolness on the field under circumstances of the most trying character.

Captain Critchlow was born in Tonawanda, N.Y., in 1867, and is only 32 years of age. He attended the Rochester University and after graduating from that institution went to the University of Pennsylvania, where he studied medicine for several years, graduating in 1894 with the degree of M.D. For the next year and a half he was in the German hospital at Philadelphia, where he was enabled to obtain a practical insight into the mysteries of *materia medica*, and upon leaving there he came to this city, where his brother, E. B. Critchlow, a prominent attorney, was already established in business.

Dr. Critchlow became a member of the National Guard some time after his arrival, being attached to the medical staff with the rank of first lieutenant. He proved to be a valuable and efficient member, always on the alert and endeared himself to all his associates.

When the call was made for troops he enlisted in Battery B and was made a second lieutenant in that organization.

His services in the Philippines were valuable. On the night attack of the Spanish it was Lieutenant Critchlow who brought the ammunition to the firing line at the time when it was most needed. In every place to which he was assigned he was always at the fore and his conspicuous bravery was the subject of special commendation, as has been related. Upon the promotion of Captain Grant to the rank of major, he was advanced to that of captain, coming home in command of the organization with which he went out as a second lieutenant.

LIEUTENANT GEORGE W. GIBBS

First Lieutenant George W. Gibbs of Battery A is a well-known character in this State, in Montana and in Massachusetts, his old home, where he was born. His father was a veteran of the War of the Rebellion and George was a member of the order in Montana, having been department commander with the rank of colonel. He has always been interested in matters appertaining to the National Guard; was a member of an infantry regiment in Massachusetts, a captain of a troop of cavalry in Montana and captain of Battery A, N.G.U., and major of the battalion at the outbreak of hostilities with Spain.

He was at one time chief of the fire department in Helena and was a member of the Salt Lake City department at the time W. A. Stanton was its chief, being captain of the chemical. He afterwards served as Deputy Sheriff when Harvey Hardy was at the head of that department.

Gibbs is forty-one years of age and married. Two children, a boy and a girl, are the result of a union with a most estimable lady.

Prior to coming to this city and before he went to Montana he was in Colorado, where he was employed as a sheriff's officer, serving with distinction. He spent some time in San Francisco, where he was in the employ of one of the leading traction companies.

LIEUTENANT RAYMOND C. NAYLOR

Lieutenant Raymond C. Naylor was born in Salt Lake City in 1873. His early education was received in the public schools of Utah. Later he attended the University of Utah, from which he graduated with honour. As a student he took a prominent part in athletics and military training, being a member of the baseball team as well as captain of one of the companies of students then taking military drill under Lieutenant Wright. He afterward taught school for several years and was engaged in that labour in Centerville when the war broke out. Those who knew him well were not surprised when he stepped to the front and offered his service to his country along with others who were willing to brave any peril in defence of their country's honour. Lieutenant Naylor had long associated himself with the National Guard, in which he was captain for two years. He afterwards was promoted major and at the breaking out of hostilities he was filling the office of assistant inspector general with the rank of lieutenant-colonel.

When the batteries were organized Governor Wells appointed him a second lieutenant of Battery A, which position he filled with such distinction that he was promoted first lieutenant.

As an officer Lieutenant Naylor won the respect and admiration of both officers and men. His interest in behalf of the privates gained for him a popularity which was not surpassed by any of the officers in the batteries.

LIEUTENANT ORRIN R. GROW

Second Lieutenant Orrin R. Grow, the youngest commissioned officer of the Utah batteries at the time of their departure for the Philippines, was born in Salt Lake City October 20, 1873. As a boy he received his education in the public schools of Salt Lake City and afterwards he attended the University of Utah several years, but he did not remain long enough to graduate. While at the University he took military training under Lieutenant Wright and after leaving that institution he joined the Denhalter Rifles as bugler. He soon was promoted sergeant and subsequently lieutenant.

When the Denhalters joined the National Guard in 1892 Mr. Grow went with them and was unanimously chosen captain of Company A, First Infantry, N.G.U. Later he was chosen major, a position which he held with credit until the breaking out of hostilities. His ability was recognized by Governor Wells, who appointed him a second lieutenant of Battery B when that organization was mustered in. Lieutenant Grow went with his battery to the Philippines, and during the fighting at Malate distinguished himself. During January, 1899, he returned home owing to serious illness. His early departure from the island prevented him from winning greater honours in the insurrection, as his ability was displayed in the Spanish-American war.

LIEUTENANT WILLIAM C. WEBB

Along with the many native sons of Utah who joined the ranks in defence of their country there were some who were born on foreign soil. Such a man was Lieutenant William C. Webb, who was born in England March 13, 1873. In his early youth Webb attended the schools of his native country and while he was yet a youth he accompanied his parents when they emigrated to Utah.

Lieutenant Webb early associated himself with military affairs, as he was a member of the Denhalter Rifles, and when that organization lost its identity in the National Guard he became one of the most active workers in the new service. When Captain Grow of Company A became major of the First Battalion, First Infantry, N.G.U., Webb was unanimously chosen captain of that company. He held this position until he was appointed a second lieutenant of Battery A by Governor Wells.

When the Utah volunteers left for Manila Lieutenant Webb accompanied them. He took part in the Malate campaign, where he showed promise of that brilliant work which he later accomplished in the Filipino outbreak. At the breaking out of the insurrection he had charge of the left platoon of Battery A at Santa Mesa hill. His fearlessness and daring at that place won for him the universal admiration of his men. Later he was placed in command of the river gunboat *Cavadonga*, and during all the fierce fighting of that little boat he manipulated her with remarkable skill.

Lieutenant Webb, on account of his exceptional work, was recommended for a Lieutenancy in the regular army, a position which he will undoubtedly accept.

Lieutenant George A. Seaman

Lieutenant George A. Seaman, who went away as a corporal of Battery A, and came back with the "straps" of a second lieutenant, was born in the little town of Morgan, twenty-nine years ago. While he was yet a boy his parents moved to Ogden, where he secured the foundation of the education which was later enlarged upon at the State University. He remained at that institution four years, graduating with honour in 1892. While obtaining his mental training he was a member of the University Battalion, in which organization he acquitted himself so well that his name was placed upon the honorary roll at Washington. It was also during his college career that he became acquainted with Miss Lottie Fox, daughter of Jesse W. Fox. Between them sprang up a mutual attachment, which was later consummated at the altar. Shortly afterwards Lieutenant Seaman moved with his wife to Bountiful, where he took up school teaching as a profession. He showed an efficiency in his work which won the esteem of all his patrons and pupils. When the call for soldiers was made his blood was of that order which impelled him to drop the master's rod and take up the sword in defence of his country.

Having enlisted he set to work to familiarizing himself with all the tactics pertaining to artillery warfare, and soon made himself acquainted with military science. His studious habits and his morality soon commended him to his superior officers who recommended him for the first vacancy which occurred. He was appointed second lieutenant of Battery B, which position he held with honour until the mustering out of the battalion.

LIEUTENANT FRANK T. HINES

Lieutenant Frank T. Hines, the son of Mr. and Mrs. Frank L. Hines, was born twenty-one years ago in Salt Lake City. He attended the city schools from which he graduated in 1896. For several years thereafter he was employed at Mercur and later entered the Agricultural College. It was while at the college that Mr. Hines learned to like the military life which he subsequently led for a short period.

When the country called for volunteers he enlisted in Captain Grant's battery as a private, but he was soon appointed duty sergeant. The latter position he filled very creditably and when a vacancy occurred by reason of the resignation of Lieutenant Grow, he was elevated to the Second Lieutenancy, which office he held until the batteries were discharged.

LIEUTENANT JOHN A. ANDERSON

Lieutenant John A. Anderson, one of the few who worked his way up by sheer force of ability, was born in Smithfield, Cache county, Utah, twenty-five years ago. He received his education in the district school of his native town, and later went to work as a millman, the occupation which he followed at the breaking out of the war.

When the batteries went away he was a duty sergeant of Battery B, in which capacity he earned the position which he afterwards secured. It was Sergeant Anderson who had charge of that section of the Utah Battalion which accompanied General Lawton in his expedition in the interior as far as San Isidro. Following his return he was appointed first sergeant of Battery B, and just before the organization left the island he received his commission as second lieutenant. Lieutenant Anderson was a brave, efficient man, and one who won the respect of all who knew him.

SERGEANT HARRY A. YOUNG

Sergeant Harry A. Young, son of the late Lorenzo D. Young, was born in Salt Lake City February 24, 1865. During his boyhood he attended the public school of his native town, and afterwards he spent several years in the Utah University, where he evinced a great liking to medicine. During 1884-85 he filled a mission to the Northern States. Soon after his return he went East and entered the medical department of Columbia College. He graduated from this institution with distinguished honours and great future promise to his profession. He established himself in Salt Lake City, where he succeeded in building up quite an extensive practice in a short time. The blood of a patriot flowed through the veins of Dr. Young and when his country needed his service he cheerfully joined the ranks and was appointed quartermaster-sergeant of Battery A, a position which he filled with great credit. When the Utah volunteers embarked for Manila Sergeant Young went with them and took part in the fighting against the Spaniards. Although his service as a doctor was not required, Dr. Young was continually in the front administering to the wants of the wounded men. Subsequently he participated in the fighting of the Tagalan outbreak, and it was while he was bravely at the front in search of opportunities to perform deeds of mercy that he met with his death at the hand of the enemy on February 6, 1899.

Those who were intimately acquainted with Dr. Young knew his sterling worth and admired his manhood. He ever walked in the path of right, unmindful of the opinions of the world. What he considered to be his duty he did with unswerving honesty. He was diligent and studious and applied himself with untiring energy to his books. As a soldier the batterymen will remember his unceasing efforts to better their condition. During the five tedious months of barrack life when others were idly waiting, he devoted himself to his chosen profession. Had Sergeant Harry A. Young lived two days longer he would have received his commission as a surgeon in the United States army.

SERGEANT FORD FISHER

Sergeant Ford Fisher, who bravely gave up his life in his country's defence, was born at Seaford, Delaware, twenty-three years ago. He was the son of I. M. Fisher of Salt Lake City. At an early age Ford, as he was better known among his associates, came to Salt Lake City with his parents. Here he attended the city High School, from which he graduated with high honours. While at the High School he was noted for his efficiency in mathematics and here he developed a liking for civil engineering, which he later studied at the Washington State University. For some time prior to the breaking out of hostilities with Spain he had associated himself with the National Guard, and when the President's call came too much patriotic blood flowed through his veins to admit of any second appeal, and he enlisted with the batteries.

Major Young soon became acquainted with the young man's military ability and he was appointed drill sergeant at Camp Kent.

When the batteries departed for the Philippines he went with them and distinguished himself for his gallantry in the Malate campaign. Later during the insurrection he took part with the other Utah men in many a fierce conflict with the insurgents until he was stricken down by the enemy's bullet while heroically defending his position at San Luiz on May 14, 1899.

The Utah artillerymen remember the stalwart figure of Sergeant Fisher as it loomed up in the forefront at Santa Mesa, Mariquina and Sexmoan. He was an inspiration to the wavering spirits of the Utahn in twenty hard encounters. His voice ever sounded as a note of cheer and his ringing command never failed to infuse with new life. Always attending to his duties he expected the same of others; his soul was too great to stoop to the level of anything base; his heart was honest and open and free. He was a pleasant companion and a true friend. He was blessed with an abundance of original humour which made him doubly loved by the soldiers during the lonely hours of barrack life.

At the time of his death Sergeant Fisher was first in line of promotion, as he had been recommended for the next commission by Major Young.

Roster

BATTALION UTAH LIGHT ARTILLERY, U. S. V.

*Major Frank A. Grant, Commanding.

BATTERY A.

OFFICERS.

Captain, E. A. WEDGEWOOD.................................Salt Lake City
  Wounded April 23, 1899.
First Lieutenant, GEORGE W. GIBBS....................Salt Lake City
Second Lieutenant, WILLIAM C. WEBB................Salt Lake City
Second Lieutenant, JOHN A. ANDERSON..........................Logan

SERGEANTS.

First, JOSEPH O. NYSTROM............................Salt Lake City
Quartermaster, ADNEBYTH L. WILLIAMS.............Salt Lake City
Veterinary, JOHN H. MEREDITH............................Kaysville
EMIL LEHMAN ....Salt Lake City
EMIL V. JOHNSON.....................................Salt Lake City
ARTHUR W. BROWN....................................Salt Lake City
WILLIAM E. KNEAS...................................Salt Lake City
CHARLES R. MABEY...Bountiful
MARK E. BEZZANT....................................Pleasant Grove

CORPORALS.

GEO. S. BACKMAN....................................Salt Lake City
NOBLE A. McDONNEL.................................Salt Lake City
WM. JACOBSON ....Salt Lake City
NELSON E. MARGETTS................................Salt Lake City
THOMAS COLLINS ....Salt Lake City
WM. NELSON, JR.....................................Salt Lake City
JOHN R. WOOLSEY...Kaysville
PETER JENSEN ....Newton
SAMUEL HESBURG ....Salt Lake City
LINDSEY HUDSON ....Salt Lake City
EDWARD G. WOOD ....Logan
LEONARD DUFFIN ....Salt Lake City

*Major Richard W. Young, who originally commanded the battalion, resigned to become Associate Justice of the Supreme Court of the Philippines and Major Frank A. Grant superceded him as commander of the batteries.

HENRY L. SOUTHER...Mercur
    Wounded March 24, 1899.
DON C. JOHNSON ....Springville
FRANK H. COULTER ....Ogden
JAS. W. MERANDA ....Eureka
JAMES M. DUNN.....................................Tooele
JNO. FLANNIGAN ....Mammoth
RICHARD L. BUSH......................................Logan
GEORGE WILLIAMS ....Salt Lake City
FRANK J. UTZ.......................................Mercur
STEPHEN BJARNSON............................Spanish Fork
PHILLIP SCHOEBER ....Salina
WILLARD H. FARNES..........................Salt Lake City
FRANK WICKERSHAM...........................Salt Lake City

ARTIFICERS.

FRANK DILLINGHAM ....Eureka
LEE A. CURTIS.......................................Ogden

WAGONER.

ANTONE LITJEROTH ....Provo

MUSICIANS.

JOSEPH WESSLER ....
MORTON T. GOODWIN...........................Heber City

PRIVATES.

ABPLANALP, JOHN D...................................Heber
    Wounded April 24, 1899.
ACKARET, MAHLON H.................................Ogden
ALEXANDER, ROBERT ....Salt Lake City
ANDERSON, DAVID M................................Peterson
ANDERSON, PETER ....Richfield
AUSTIN, BERT W.....................................Bingham
BAKER, JOHN ....Eureka
BEESLEY, JOHN W...................................Provo
BENZON, GLENN ....Salt Lake City
BILLINGS, CLAUD G...................................Eureka
BJARNSON, EINER.............................Spanish Fork
BORKMAN, ARTHUR ....Mercur
BRAMAN, JOHN ....Bingham
    Wounded April 26, 1899.
BRIDGMAN, JOHN D.........................Salt Lake City
BURTON, RAY S. ....Salt Lake City
CARR, JOSEPH W.....................................Ogden
CARLSON, GUST...........................Salt Lake City
CHAMBERLIN, VIRGIL L..............................Ogden

CHATLIN, EUGENE ....Castle Gate
CHAFFIN, MILLARD ....Salt Lake City
CHRISTENSEN, THEODORE ....Salt Lake City
COLLETT, RALPH ....Salt Lake City
COLLINS, WM. J..Salt Lake City
CONOVER ROBT. F..Provo
CORAY, DON R..Provo
CRAGER, FRED H..............................Salt Lake City
DALGETY, JOHN ....Eureka
DALIMORE, PHILLIP ....Lehi
DUNCAN, ELMER ....Heber
DECKER, LEO ....Salt Lake City
DOYLE, JOSEPH ....Mammoth
DUNNING, DANIEL A..Provo
EDDY, LOUIS B...Eureka
ELLIS, ALFRED ....Silver City
EVANS, WILLARD ....Salt Lake City
FOWLER, GEORGE ....Salt Lake City
FORCELAND, CHARLES G......................Salt Lake City
GRAVES, NED C....................................Salt Lake City
GREEN, LOREN C............................American Fork
HALL, PARKER J..Ogden
  Wounded March 25, 1899.
HALL, WALTER S....................................West Portage
HARDIE, FRANCIS R..............................Salt Lake City
HEATHERLY, CHARLES ....Salt Lake City
HERBERTZ, PETER ....Castle Gate
HOGAN, JOHN ....Ogden
HAGGAN, THOMAS A., JR....................................Manti
HOLDAWAY, PARLEY P......................................Provo
HOBKINS, EVERITT E.......................................Provo
HUBERT, WELMER E.............................Salt Lake City
HUGHES, JOHN W..Eureka
JENSEN, HANS ....Hyde Park
KELL, JOHN V...Eureka
KLENKE, HENDRECH ....Salt Lake City
KING, SAMUEL ....Eureka
KNAUSS, WM. G....................................Salt Lake City
LARSEN, G. R. ....Manti
LAWSON, D. V...Joseph
LEONARD, THOMAS ....Eureka
LEWIS, SAMUEL C...............................Salt Lake City
MARTIN, FRED S....................................Salt Lake City
McCABE, JAMES ....Eureka
McCARTY, LEONARD....................................Manti

111

OHMER, ARTHUR F............................Rawlins, Wyoming
PERRET, WILLIAM E...........................Salt Lake City
PETERSON, CHARLES ....Salt Lake City
PETERSON, FRANK C..................................Ogden
PETERSON LOUIS C............................Salt Lake City
PHILLIPS, MANNIE C...........................Salt Lake City
QUINN, JAMES ....Park City
RADEMACHER, AUGUST ....Ogden
RASMUSSEN, SEVEREN ....Park City
RAUSCHER, EDWARD W..................................Nephi
RICHMOND, WILLIAM ....Provo
ROBINSON, WILLIAM J..............................Park City
ROBISON, JOHN L.........................Pleasant Grove
RYAN, MICHAEL F...... ....Salt Lake City
RYVER, WILLIAM A.... ....Salt Lake City
SELMER, EMIL F.............................Salt Lake City
    Wounded April 26, 1899.
SLEATER, HAROLD E..........................Salt Lake City
SMITH, THOMAS R.....................................Logan
SORENSON, HANS ....Salt Lake City
SORENSON, JOSEPH F.........................Salt Lake City
SORENSON, KNUD ....Eureka
STATEN, STANLEY ....Springville
STOUT, CHARLES S...........................Salt Lake City
TIPTON, WILLIAM ....Springville
TOMPKINS, ODELL D..........................Mystic, Conn.
TRIPP, FRANCIS B...........................Salt Lake City
VINCENT, FRANK A..........................Salt Lake City
WALQUIST, CHARLES A.......................Salt Lake City
WEBER, GEORGE E...............................Park City
WILLIAMS, ALBERT R........................Salt Lake City
WONNACOTT, JAMES E.......................Salt Lake City
WYCHERLEY, SAMUEL A.........................Coalville
WYNE, HOMER W.............................Salt Lake City
ZAHLER, JOHN F....................................Bountiful

HONORABLY DISCHARGED.

First Sergeant, D. H. WELLS.......................Salt Lake City
    October 31, 1898.
Sergeant, A. L. ROBINSON..........................Mt. Pleasant
    April 3, 1899.
Corporal, WILLARD CALL................................Bountiful
    December 14, 1898.
Corporal, LEWIS P. HANSON........................Salt Lake City
    June 28, 1899.
Corporal, WM. D. RITER...........................Salt Lake City
    October 31, 1898.

Corporal, JOHN B. ROGERS............................Salt Lake City
June 29, 1899.
Corporal, GEO. A. SEAMAN..............................Bountiful
November 21, 1898.
Corporal, FRANK B. SHELLY..........................Salt Lake City
June 28, 1899.
Farrier, W. M. CLAWSON................................Kaysville
May 18, 1899.
Farrier, H. P. HANSEN..............................Salt Lake City
June 28, 1899.
Artificer, V. A. SMITH..............................Salt Lake City
June 28, 1899.
Private, ETHAN E. ALLEN............................Salt Lake City
June 28, 1899.
Private, WM. W. BURNETT.........................San Jose, Cal.
February 24, 1899.
Private, A. C. CAFFALL..............................Salt Lake City
July 7, 1899.
Private, THEO. CLEGHORN............................Salt Lake City
May 11, 1899.
Private, JAS. W. CONNELL...........................Salt Lake City
April 10, 1899.
Private, A. H. FICHTNER............................Salt Lake City
June 28, 1899.
Private, P. B. FREDERICKSON..............................Eureka
June 28, 1899.
Private, GEORGE GRANTHAM.....................American Fork
June 28, 1899.
Private, JOSEPH J. HOLBROOK......................Bountiful
December 14, 1898.
Private, ELMER JOHNSON............................Salt Lake City
June 28, 1899
Private, J. B. LICKLEDERER.........................Salt Lake City
July 7, 1899.
Private, HERBERT L. MEYERS...................San Francisco, Cal.
June 28, 1899.
Private, ISAAC E. LITTRELL.........................Berkeley, Cal.
June 28, 1899.
Private, THEODORE NEWMAN.......................Salt Lake City
April 10, 1899.
Private, FRANK E. PETERS............................Salt Lake City
June 28, 1899.
Private, W. I. ROWLAND...............................Salt Lake City
February 1, 1899.
Private, ISAAC RUSSELL..............................Salt Lake City
January 18, 1899.
Private, BISMARCK SNYDER............................Park City
December 14, 1898.
Private, A. L. THOMAS, JR..........................Salt Lake City
June 12, 1898.
Private, JOHN A. TILSON............................Salt Lake City
June 28, 1899.
Private, FRANCIS TUTTLE...............................Bountiful
September 21, 1898.
Private, CHAS. E. VARIAN ....Salt Lake City
December 14, 1898.

113

Private, E. P. WALKER...................................Salt Lake City
June 28, 1899.

ROLL OF HONOR.

KILLED IN ACTION.

Quartermaster-Sergeant, HARRY A. YOUNG.............Salt Lake City
February 6, 1899.
Sergeant, FORD FISHER...........................Salt Lake City
May 14, 1899.
Corporal, JOHN G. YOUNG.........................Salt Lake City
February 5, 1899.
Private, WILHELM G. GOODMAN.....................Salt Lake City
February 5, 1899.

DIED OF DISEASE.

Corporal, GEORGE O. LARSON...............................Dover
December 10, 1898.
Corporal, JOHN T. KENNEDY.............................Park City
March 15, 1899.
Private, OSCAR A. FENINGER............................Park City
June 5, 1899.
Private, CHARLES PARSONS........................Salt Lake City
April 20, 1899.

BATTERY B.

OFFICERS.

Captain, JOHN F. CRITCHLOW.....................Salt Lake City

First Lieutenant, RAYMOND C. NAYLOR..............Salt Lake City

Second Lieutenant, GEORGE A. SEAMAN...............Bountiful
Wounded April 11, 1899.

Second Lieutenant, FRANK T. HINES (Batt. Adjt.)....Salt Lake City

SERGEANTS.

First, JOHN U. BUCHI.......................................Provo

Quartermaster, JAMES K. BURCH............................Ogden

Veterinary, FELIX BACHMAN................................Provo

LOUIS N. FEHR.....................................Salt Lake City

ROBERT STEWART ....Plain City

JOHN A. BOSHARD ....Provo

GEORGE B. WARDLAW ....Ogden
Wounded February 4, 1899.

ANDREW PETERSON, JR.....................................Manti
Wounded March 11, 1899.

HARVEY DUSENBERRY ....Provo

CORPORALS.

JAMES J. RYAN ....Mercur

CHARLES C. CLAPPER.....................................Mercur

THEODORE L. GENTER.............................Salt Lake City

NEPHI OTTESON ....Manti

114

HENRY L. SOUTHER.......................................Mercur
  Wounded March 24, 1899.
DON C. JOHNSON ....Springville
FRANK H. COULTER ....Ogden
JAS. W. MERANDA ....Eureka
JAMES M. DUNN...Tooele
JNO. FLANNIGAN ....Mammoth
RICHARD L. BUSH........ ....Logan
GEORGE WILLIAMS ....Salt Lake City
FRANK J. UTZ............. ... .'.....Mercur
STEPHEN BJARNSON............. ....,Spanish Fork
PHILLIP SCHOEBER ....Salina
WILLARD H. FARNES...............................Salt Lake City
FRANK WICKERSHAM................................Salt Lake City

ARTIFICERS.

FRANK DILLINGHAM ....Eureka
LEE A. CURTIS...Ogden

WAGONER.

ANTONE LITJEROTH ....Provo

MUSICIANS.

JOSEPH WESSLER ....
MORTON T. GOODWIN................................Heber City

PRIVATES.

ABPLANALP, JOHN D....................................Heber
  Wounded April 24, 1899.
ACKARET, MAHLON H...................................Ogden
ALEXANDER, ROBERT ....Salt Lake City
ANDERSON, DAVID M....... ....Peterson
ANDERSON, PETER ....Richfield
AUSTIN, BERT W..Bingham
BAKER, JOHN ....Eureka
BEESLEY, JOHN W... ....Provo
BENZON, GLENN ....Salt Lake City
BILLINGS, CLAUD G....................................Eureka
BJARNSON, EINER...... .. ..Spanish Fork
BORKMAN, ARTHUR ....Mercur
BRAMAN, JOHN ....Bingham
  Wounded April 26, 1899.
BRIDGMAN, JOHN D...............................Salt Lake City
BURTON, RAY S. ....Salt Lake City
CARR, JOSEPH W..Ogden
CARLSON, GUST...................................Salt Lake City
CHAMBERLIN, VIRGIL L................................Ogden

115

```
CHATLIN, EUGENE .............................Castle Gate
CHAFFIN, MILLARD ...........................Salt Lake City
CHRISTENSEN, THEODORE .....................Salt Lake City
COLLETT, RALPH .............................Salt Lake City
COLLINS, WM. J..............................Salt Lake City
CONOVER ROBT. F..................................Provo
CORAY, DON R.....................................Provo
CRAGER, FRED H.............................Salt Lake City
DALGETY, JOHN ....................................Eureka
DALIMORE, PHILLIP ...............................Lehi
DUNCAN, ELMER ...................................Heber
DECKER, LEO ...............................Salt Lake City
DOYLE, JOSEPH ...................................Mammoth
DUNNING, DANIEL A................................Provo
EDDY, LOUIS B....................................Eureka
ELLIS, ALFRED .................................Silver City
EVANS, WILLARD ............................Salt Lake City
FOWLER, GEORGE ............................Salt Lake City
FORCELAND, CHARLES G.......................Salt Lake City
GRAVES, NED C..............................Salt Lake City
GREEN, LOREN C..............................American Fork
HALL, PARKER J....................................Ogden
     Wounded March 25, 1899.
HALL, WALTER S..............................West Portage
HARDIE, FRANCIS R..........................Salt Lake City
HEATHERLY, CHARLES ........................Salt Lake City
HERBERTZ, PETER ...........................Castle Gate
HOGAN, JOHN ......................................Ogden
HAGGAN, THOMAS A., JR............................Manti
HOLDAWAY, PARLEY P...............................Provo
HOBKINS, EVERITT E...............................Provo
HUBERT, WELMER E...........................Salt Lake City
HUGHES, JOHN W...................................Eureka
JENSEN, HANS ..................................Hyde Park
KELL, JOHN V.....................................Eureka
KLENKE, HENDRECH ..........................Salt Lake City
KING, SAMUEL ....................................Eureka
KNAUSS, WM. G..............................Salt Lake City
LARSEN, G. R. ...................................Manti
LAWSON, D. V....................................Joseph
LEONARD, THOMAS .................................Eureka
LEWIS, SAMUEL C............................Salt Lake City
MARTIN, FRED S.............................Salt Lake City
McCABE, JAMES ...................................Eureka
McCARTY, LEONARD.................................Manti
```

McCUBBIN, WILLIAM ....Salt Lake City
MOIR, GEORGE ....Salt Lake City
MORTON, JOHN W......................................Provo
MORTON, MILTON ....Provo
NEILSON, ANDREW P..............................Spanish Fork
NORRIS, JOHN D.................................Denver, Colorado
OLSEN, PETER ....Logan
OLSEN, REINHART ....Milton
PENNINGTON, LOUIS P..............................Brigham
PRATT, ERNEST M..............................Salt Lake City
QUICK, MARSHALL ....Provo
RAE, ALEX. ....Provo
RAE, WILLIAM ....Provo
REEDALL, THOMAS ....Salt Lake City
REES, GEORGE ....Silver City
REID, ROBERT ....Salt Lake City
ROBERTS, EDWARD J.............................Salt Lake City
ROWLAND, GEORGE E...................................Eureka
SAVAGE, WM. H......................................Eureka
SCHAUPP, FREW W.....................................Eureka
SCOTT, HYRUM C......................................Provo
SHEARER, WM. H...............................Salt Lake City
SMITH, JEROME ....Tooele
SMITH, SIDNEY J...............................Salt Lake City
SMITH, HARRY ....Salt Lake City
SNOW, JUNIUS C.....................................Provo
SNYDER, HARRY S.....................................Provo
TATE, JNO. P.......................................Tooele
TAYLOR, GEORGE ....Eureka
TURNER, MORONI ....Heber
TYREE, SAMUEL P.....................................Ogden
VANCE, JOHN R......................................Eureka
VAN SYCKLE, BENJ....................................Ogden
WALTERS, ALBERT N..................................Ogden
WALTERS, JOSEPH W..................................Ogden
WINKLER, JOSEPH G.............................Salt Lake City
WRIGHT, WILLIAM A.............................Salt Lake City
YATES, JAMES K....................................Diamond
WHEELER, GEORGE ....Ogden
ZOLLINGER, JOHN D..............................Providence

HONORABLY DISCHARGED.

Second Lieutenant, ORRIN R. GROW.....................Salt Lake City
First Sergeant, J. A. ANDERSON.............................Logan
   Discharged June 29, to accept commission as Second Lieutenant.

Quartermaster-Sergeant, CHAS. ASPLUND............ ......Fairview
    June 23, 1899.
Sergeant, ALBERT ST. MORRIS.........................Salt Lake City
    June 28, 1899.
Sergeant, HORACE E. COOLIDGE.............................Manti
    March 22, 1899.
Corporal, WM. Q. ANDERSON....... .. ..Logan
    Wounded August 24, 1898.
    December 15, 1898.
Corporal, JOHN T. DONNELLAN.... ....Salt Lake City
    March 17, 1899.
Corporal, JACOB A. HEISS.............................Salt Lake City
    December 1, 1898.
Corporal, E. V. DE MONTALVO. ....Mercur
    January 21, 1899.
Musician, JOS. F. GRANT...........................Salt Lake City
    January 11, 1899.
Saddler, LOUIS MILLER..... ....Ogden
    November 15, 1898.
Farrier, FRED D. SWEET....... ....Ogden
    April 11, 1899.
Private, GODFREY J. BLUTH....................,.Ogden
    February 12, 1899.
Private, F. D. CHATTERTON.................Salt Lake City
    January 21, 1899.
Private, JASPER D. CURTIS........... .. ..Eureka
    June 23, 1899.
Private, ROSEY P. FLORANCE.............................Ogden
    December 20, 1898.
Private, CHARLES S. HILL..............................Wellington
    June 28, 1899.
Private, BARR W. MUSSER.........................Salt Lake City
    January 17, 1899.
Private, JOHN A. PENDER................ ....Ogden
    Wounded March 30, 1899.
    May 5, 1899.
Private, THOMAS SHULL.................................Mammoth
    June 28, 1899.
Private, THOS. W. THORNBURG.'..............................Ogden
    June 28, 1899.
Private, FREDERICK BLAKE.........................Salt Lake City
    June 28, 1899.
Private, AUGUSTUS BRANSCOM......... .. ..Ogden
    June 28, 1899.
Private, WILLIAM CROOKS...............................Eureka
    June 28, 1899.
Private, JOHN FERGUSON...............................Park City
    January 15, 1899.
Private, CHAS. I. FOX...............................Salt Lake City
    June 28, 1899.
Private, GEORGE LACEY.... ....Manti
    January 10, 1899.
Private, DON C. MUSSER.............................Salt Lake City
    January 17, 1899.
Private, NEPHI REESE.................................Silver City
    November 11, 1898.

Private, GEO. SIMMONS...............................Salt Lake City
    June 23, 1899.
Private, CHRIS WAGNER...............................Salt Lake City
    March 13, 1899.
Private, CARLOS YOUNG....................... ....Salt Lake City
    June 23, 1899.

ROLL OF HONOR.

KILLED IN ACTION.

Corporal, MORITZ C. JENSEN...........................Castle Gate
    April 26, 1899.
Private, FREDERICK BUMILLER......................Salt Lake City
    April 26, 1899.
Private, MAX MADISON ....Mercur
    April 25, 1899.
Private, GEO. H. HUDSON............................... ..Mercur
    August 25, 1898.

DIED OF DISEASE.

Private, RICHARD H. RALPH....................... ....Eureka
    July 21, 1899.

LEONAUR

ALSO FROM LEONAUR
AVAILABLE IN SOFTCOVER OR HARDCOVER WITH DUST JACKET

THE 2ND MAORI WAR: 1860-1861 *by Robert Carey*—The Second Maori War, or First Taranaki War, one more bloody instalment of the conflicts between European settlers and the indigenous Maori people.

A JOURNAL OF THE SECOND SIKH WAR *by Daniel A. Sandford*—The Experiences of an Ensign of the 2nd Bengal European Regiment During the Campaign in the Punjab, India, 1848-49.

THE LIGHT INFANTRY OFFICER *by John H. Cooke*—The Experiences of an Officer of the 43rd Light Infantry in America During the War of 1812.

BUSHVELDT CARBINEERS *by George Witton*—The War Against the Boers in South Africa and the 'Breaker' Morant Incident.

LAKE'S CAMPAIGNS IN INDIA *by Hugh Pearse*—The Second Anglo Maratha War, 1803-1807.

BRITAIN IN AFGHANISTAN 1: THE FIRST AFGHAN WAR 1839-42 *by Archibald Forbes*—From invasion to destruction-a British military disaster.

BRITAIN IN AFGHANISTAN 2: THE SECOND AFGHAN WAR 1878-80 *by Archibald Forbes*—This is the history of the Second Afghan War-another episode of British military history typified by savagery, massacre, siege and battles.

UP AMONG THE PANDIES *by Vivian Dering Majendie*—Experiences of a British Officer on Campaign During the Indian Mutiny, 1857-1858.

MUTINY: 1857 *by James Humphries*—Authentic Voices from the Indian Mutiny-First Hand Accounts of Battles, Sieges and Personal Hardships.

BLOW THE BUGLE, DRAW THE SWORD *by W. H. G. Kingston*—The Wars, Campaigns, Regiments and Soldiers of the British & Indian Armies During the Victorian Era, 1839-1898.

WAR BEYOND THE DRAGON PAGODA *by Major J. J. Snodgrass*—A Personal Narrative of the First Anglo-Burmese War 1824 - 1826.

THE HERO OF ALIWAL *by James Humphries*—The Campaigns of Sir Harry Smith in India, 1843-1846, During the Gwalior War & the First Sikh War.

ALL FOR A SHILLING A DAY *by Donald F. Featherstone*—The story of H.M. 16th, the Queen's Lancers During the first Sikh War 1845-1846.

LEONAUR

ALSO FROM LEONAUR
AVAILABLE IN SOFTCOVER OR HARDCOVER WITH DUST JACKET

OFFICERS & GENTLEMEN *by Peter Hawker & William Graham*—Two Accounts of British Officers During the Peninsula War: Officer of Light Dragoons by Peter Hawker & Campaign in Portugal and Spain by William Graham .

THE WALCHEREN EXPEDITION *by Anonymous*—The Experiences of a British Officer of the 81st Regt. During the Campaign in the Low Countries of 1809.

LADIES OF WATERLOO *by Charlotte A. Eaton, Magdalene de Lancey & Juana Smith*—The Experiences of Three Women During the Campaign of 1815: Waterloo Days by Charlotte A. Eaton, A Week at Waterloo by Magdalene de Lancey & Juana's Story by Juana Smith.

JOURNAL OF AN OFFICER IN THE KING'S GERMAN LEGION *by John Frederick Hering*—Recollections of Campaigning During the Napoleonic Wars.

JOURNAL OF AN ARMY SURGEON IN THE PENINSULAR WAR *by Charles Boutflower*—The Recollections of a British Army Medical Man on Campaign During the Napoleonic Wars.

ON CAMPAIGN WITH MOORE AND WELLINGTON *by Anthony Hamilton*—The Experiences of a Soldier of the 43rd Regiment During the Peninsular War.

THE ROAD TO AUSTERLITZ *by R. G. Burton*—Napoleon's Campaign of 1805.

SOLDIERS OF NAPOLEON *by A. J. Doisy De Villargennes & Arthur Chuquet*—The Experiences of the Men of the French First Empire: Under the Eagles by A. J. Doisy De Villargennes & Voices of 1812 by Arthur Chuquet .

INVASION OF FRANCE, 1814 *by F. W. O. Maycock*—The Final Battles of the Napoleonic First Empire.

LEIPZIG—A CONFLICT OF TITANS *by Frederic Shoberl*—A Personal Experience of the 'Battle of the Nations' During the Napoleonic Wars, October 14th-19th, 1813.

SLASHERS *by Charles Cadell*—The Campaigns of the 28th Regiment of Foot During the Napoleonic Wars by a Serving Officer.

BATTLE IMPERIAL *by Charles William Vane*—The Campaigns in Germany & France for the Defeat of Napoleon 1813-1814.

SWIFT & BOLD *by Gibbes Rigaud*—The 60th Rifles During the Peninsula War.

LEONAUR

ALSO FROM LEONAUR
AVAILABLE IN SOFTCOVER OR HARDCOVER WITH DUST JACKET

OMPTEDA OF THE KING'S GERMAN LEGION *by Christian von Ompteda*—A Hanoverian Officer on Campaign Against Napoleon.

LIEUTENANT SIMMONS OF THE 95TH (RIFLES) *by George Simmons*—Recollections of the Peninsula, South of France & Waterloo Campaigns of the Napoleonic Wars.

A HORSEMAN FOR THE EMPEROR *by Jean Baptiste Gazzola*—A Cavalryman of Napoleon's Army on Campaign Throughout the Napoleonic Wars.

SERGEANT LAWRENCE *by William Lawrence*—With the 40th Regt. of Foot in South America, the Peninsular War & at Waterloo.

CAMPAIGNS WITH THE FIELD TRAIN *by Richard D. Henegan*—Experiences of a British Officer During the Peninsula and Waterloo Campaigns of the Napoleonic Wars.

CAVALRY SURGEON *by S. D. Broughton*—On Campaign Against Napoleon in the Peninsula & South of France During the Napoleonic Wars 1812-1814.

MEN OF THE RIFLES *by Thomas Knight, Henry Curling & Jonathan Leach*—The Reminiscences of Thomas Knight of the 95th (Rifles) by Thomas Knight, Henry Curling's Anecdotes by Henry Curling & The Field Services of the Rifle Brigade from its Formation to Waterloo by Jonathan Leach.

THE ULM CAMPAIGN 1805 *by F. N. Maude*—Napoleon and the Defeat of the Austrian Army During the 'War of the Third Coalition'.

SOLDIERING WITH THE 'DIVISION' *by Thomas Garrety*—The Military Experiences of an Infantryman of the 43rd Regiment During the Napoleonic Wars.

SERGEANT MORRIS OF THE 73RD FOOT *by Thomas Morris*—The Experiences of a British Infantryman During the Napoleonic Wars-Including Campaigns in Germany and at Waterloo.

A VOICE FROM WATERLOO *by Edward Cotton*—The Personal Experiences of a British Cavalryman Who Became a Battlefield Guide and Authority on the Campaign of 1815.

NAPOLEON AND HIS MARSHALS *by J. T. Headley*—The Men of the First Empire.

LEONAUR

ALSO FROM LEONAUR
AVAILABLE IN SOFTCOVER OR HARDCOVER WITH DUST JACKET

COLBORNE: A SINGULAR TALENT FOR WAR *by John Colborne*—The Napoleonic Wars Career of One of Wellington's Most Highly Valued Officers in Egypt, Holland, Italy, the Peninsula and at Waterloo.

NAPOLEON'S RUSSIAN CAMPAIGN *by Philippe Henri de Segur*—The Invasion, Battles and Retreat by an Aide-de-Camp on the Emperor's Staff.

WITH THE LIGHT DIVISION *by John H. Cooke*—The Experiences of an Officer of the 43rd Light Infantry in the Peninsula and South of France During the Napoleonic Wars.

WELLINGTON AND THE PYRENEES CAMPAIGN VOLUME I: FROM VITORIA TO THE BIDASSOA *by F. C. Beatson*—The final phase of the campaign in the Iberian Peninsula.

WELLINGTON AND THE INVASION OF FRANCE VOLUME II: THE BIDASSOA TO THE BATTLE OF THE NIVELLE *by F. C. Beatson*—The final phase of the campaign in the Iberian Peninsula.

WELLINGTON AND THE FALL OF FRANCE VOLUME III: THE GAVES AND THE BATTLE OF ORTHEZ *by F. C. Beatson*—The final phase of the campaign in the Iberian Peninsula.

NAPOLEON'S IMPERIAL GUARD: FROM MARENGO TO WATERLOO *by J. T. Headley*—The story of Napoleon's Imperial Guard and the men who commanded them.

BATTLES & SIEGES OF THE PENINSULAR WAR *by W. H. Fitchett*—Corunna, Busaco, Albuera, Ciudad Rodrigo, Badajos, Salamanca, San Sebastian & Others.

SERGEANT GUILLEMARD: THE MAN WHO SHOT NELSON? *by Robert Guillemard*—A Soldier of the Infantry of the French Army of Napoleon on Campaign Throughout Europe.

WITH THE GUARDS ACROSS THE PYRENEES *by Robert Batty*—The Experiences of a British Officer of Wellington's Army During the Battles for the Fall of Napoleonic France, 1813 .

A STAFF OFFICER IN THE PENINSULA *by E. W. Buckham*—An Officer of the British Staff Corps Cavalry During the Peninsula Campaign of the Napoleonic Wars.

THE LEIPZIG CAMPAIGN: 1813—NAPOLEON AND THE "BATTLE OF THE NATIONS" *by F. N. Maude*—Colonel Maude's analysis of Napoleon's campaign of 1813 around Leipzig.

LEONAUR

ALSO FROM LEONAUR
AVAILABLE IN SOFTCOVER OR HARDCOVER WITH DUST JACKET

CAPTAIN COIGNET by Jean-Roch Coignet—A Soldier of Napoleon's Imperial Guard from the Italian Campaign to Russia and Waterloo.

HUSSAR ROCCA by Albert Jean Michel de Rocca—A French cavalry officer's experiences of the Napoleonic Wars and his views on the Peninsular Campaigns against the Spanish, British And Guerilla Armies.

MARINES TO 95TH (RIFLES) by Thomas Fernyhough—The military experiences of Robert Fernyhough during the Napoleonic Wars.

LIGHT BOB by Robert Blakeney—The experiences of a young officer in H.M 28th & 36th regiments of the British Infantry during the Peninsular Campaign of the Napoleonic Wars 1804 - 1814.

WITH WELLINGTON'S LIGHT CAVALRY by William Tomkinson—The Experiences of an officer of the 16th Light Dragoons in the Peninsular and Waterloo campaigns of the Napoleonic Wars.

SERGEANT BOURGOGNE by Adrien Bourgogne—With Napoleon's Imperial Guard in the Russian Campaign and on the Retreat from Moscow 1812 - 13.

SURTEES OF THE 95TH (RIFLES) by William Surtees—A Soldier of the 95th (Rifles) in the Peninsular campaign of the Napoleonic Wars.

SWORDS OF HONOUR by Henry Newbolt & Stanley L. Wood—The Careers of Six Outstanding Officers from the Napoleonic Wars, the Wars for India and the American Civil War.

ENSIGN BELL IN THE PENINSULAR WAR by George Bell—The Experiences of a young British Soldier of the 34th Regiment 'The Cumberland Gentlemen' in the Napoleonic wars.

HUSSAR IN WINTER by Alexander Gordon—A British Cavalry Officer during the retreat to Corunna in the Peninsular campaign of the Napoleonic Wars.

THE COMPLEAT RIFLEMAN HARRIS by Benjamin Harris as told to and transcribed by Captain Henry Curling, 52nd Regt. of Foot—The adventures of a soldier of the 95th (Rifles) during the Peninsular Campaign of the Napoleonic Wars.

THE ADVENTURES OF A LIGHT DRAGOON by George Farmer & G.R. Gleig—A cavalryman during the Peninsular & Waterloo Campaigns, in captivity & at the siege of Bhurtpore, India.

LEONAUR

ALSO FROM LEONAUR

AVAILABLE IN SOFTCOVER OR HARDCOVER WITH DUST JACKET

THE LIFE OF THE REAL BRIGADIER GERARD VOLUME 1—THE YOUNG HUSSAR 1782-1807 *by Jean-Baptiste De Marbot*—A French Cavalryman Of the Napoleonic Wars at Marengo, Austerlitz, Jena, Eylau & Friedland.

THE LIFE OF THE REAL BRIGADIER GERARD VOLUME 2—IMPERIAL AIDE-DE-CAMP 1807-1811 *by Jean-Baptiste De Marbot*—A French Cavalryman of the Napoleonic Wars at Saragossa, Landshut, Eckmuhl, Ratisbon, Aspern-Essling, Wagram, Busaco & Torres Vedras.

THE LIFE OF THE REAL BRIGADIER GERARD VOLUME 3—COLONEL OF CHASSEURS 1811-1815 *by Jean-Baptiste De Marbot*—A French Cavalryman in the retreat from Moscow, Lutzen, Bautzen, Katzbach, Leipzig, Hanau & Waterloo.

THE INDIAN WAR OF 1864 *by Eugene Ware*—The Experiences of a Young Officer of the 7th Iowa Cavalry on the Western Frontier During the Civil War.

THE MARCH OF DESTINY *by Charles E. Young & V. Devinny*—Dangers of the Trail in 1865 by Charles E. Young & The Story of a Pioneer by V. Devinny, two Accounts of Early Emigrants to Colorado.

CROSSING THE PLAINS *by William Audley Maxwell*—A First Hand Narrative of the Early Pioneer Trail to California in 1857.

CHIEF OF SCOUTS *by William F. Drannan*—A Pilot to Emigrant and Government Trains, Across the Plains of the Western Frontier.

THIRTY-ONE YEARS ON THE PLAINS AND IN THE MOUNTAINS *by William F. Drannan*—William Drannan was born to be a pioneer, hunter, trapper and wagon train guide during the momentous days of the Great American West.

THE INDIAN WARS VOLUNTEER *by William Thompson*—Recollections of the Conflict Against the Snakes, Shoshone, Bannocks, Modocs and Other Native Tribes of the American North West.

THE 4TH TENNESSEE CAVALRY *by George B. Guild*—The Services of Smith's Regiment of Confederate Cavalry by One of its Officers.

COLONEL WORTHINGTON'S SHILOH *by T. Worthington*—The Tennessee Campaign, 1862, by an Officer of the Ohio Volunteers.

FOUR YEARS IN THE SADDLE *by W. L. Curry*—The History of the First Regiment Ohio Volunteer Cavalry in the American Civil War.

LEONAUR

ALSO FROM LEONAUR
AVAILABLE IN SOFTCOVER OR HARDCOVER WITH DUST JACKET

ESCAPE FROM THE FRENCH *by Edward Boys*—A Young Royal Navy Midshipman's Adventures During the Napoleonic War.

THE VOYAGE OF H.M.S. PANDORA *by Edward Edwards R. N. & George Hamilton, edited by Basil Thomson*—In Pursuit of the Mutineers of the Bounty in the South Seas—1790-1791.

MEDUSA *by J. B. Henry Savigny and Alexander Correard and Charlotte-Adélaïde Dard* —Narrative of a Voyage to Senegal in 1816 & The Sufferings of the Picard Family After the Shipwreck of the Medusa.

THE SEA WAR OF 1812 VOLUME 1 *by A. T. Mahan*—A History of the Maritime Conflict.

THE SEA WAR OF 1812 VOLUME 2 *by A. T. Mahan*—A History of the Maritime Conflict.

WETHERELL OF H. M. S. HUSSAR *by John Wetherell*—The Recollections of an Ordinary Seaman of the Royal Navy During the Napoleonic Wars.

THE NAVAL BRIGADE IN NATAL *by C. R. N. Burne*—With the Guns of H. M. S. Terrible & H. M. S. Tartar during the Boer War 1899-1900.

THE VOYAGE OF H. M. S. BOUNTY *by William Bligh*—The True Story of an 18th Century Voyage of Exploration and Mutiny.

SHIPWRECK! *by William Gilly*—The Royal Navy's Disasters at Sea 1793-1849.

KING'S CUTTERS AND SMUGGLERS: 1700-1855 *by E. Keble Chatterton*—A unique period of maritime history-from the beginning of the eighteenth to the middle of the nineteenth century when British seamen risked all to smuggle valuable goods from wool to tea and spirits from and to the Continent.

CONFEDERATE BLOCKADE RUNNER *by John Wilkinson*—The Personal Recollections of an Officer of the Confederate Navy.

NAVAL BATTLES OF THE NAPOLEONIC WARS *by W. H. Fitchett*—Cape St. Vincent, the Nile, Cadiz, Copenhagen, Trafalgar & Others.

PRISONERS OF THE RED DESERT *by R. S. Gwatkin-Williams*—The Adventures of the Crew of the Tara During the First World War.

U-BOAT WAR 1914-1918 *by James B. Connolly/Karl von Schenk*—Two Contrasting Accounts from Both Sides of the Conflict at Sea D uring the Great War.